Facebook Advertising

A Complete Guide for Facebook and Instagram Advertising

Text Copyright © _____

All rights reserved. No part of this guide may be reproduced in any form without permission in writing from the publisher except in the case of brief quotations embodied in critical articles or reviews.

Legal & Disclaimer

The information contained in this book and its contents is not designed to replace or take the place of any form of medical or professional advice; and is not meant to replace the need for independent medical, financial, legal or other professional advice or services, as may be required. The content and information in this book has been provided for educational and entertainment purposes only.

The content and information contained in this book has been compiled from sources deemed reliable, and it is accurate to the best of the Author's knowledge, information and belief. However, the Author cannot guarantee its accuracy and validity and cannot be held liable for any errors and/or omissions. Further, changes are periodically made to this book as and when needed. Where appropriate and/or necessary, you must consult a professional (including but not limited to your doctor, attorney, financial advisor or such other professional advisor) before using any of the suggested remedies, techniques, or information in this book.

Upon using the contents and information contained in this book, you agree to hold harmless the Author from and against any damages, costs, and expenses, including any legal fees potentially resulting from the application of any of the information provided by this book. This disclaimer applies to any loss, damages or injury caused by the use and application, whether directly or indirectly, of any advice or information presented, whether for breach of contract, tort, negligence, personal injury, criminal intent, or under any other cause of action.

You agree to accept all risks of using the information presented in this book.

You agree that by continuing to read this book, where appropriate and/or necessary, you shall consult a professional (including but not limited to your doctor, attorney, or financial advisor or such other advisor as needed) before using any of the suggested remedies, techniques, or information in this book.

Table of Contents

Introduction 7
Part I Before the Beginning 10
  Chapter 1 – Understanding Facebook Business Manager 10
    1.1 What Is It and Why Do We Need It? 10
    1.2 How to Create a Business Manager Account 12
    1.3 What is the Structure of Business Manager? 14
    1.4 What Roles Are There?: The Difference Between Partners and People 22
    1.5 How to Add an Existing Ad Account to Business Manager 23
  Chapter 2 – How to Correctly Setup an Ad Account 26
    2.1 Payment Methods 26
    2.2 Currency 28
    2.3 Timezone: Why is it Important? 29
  Chapter 3 – What is a Key to Success in Facebook Advertising? 30
    3.1 Setting Your Goals 30
    3.2 Working with Strategy: Facebook Ads Funnel 31
    3.3 Knowing Your Target Audience 35
    3.4 Effectively Using Target Instruments 36
Part II – 4 Steps to Create Advertisement in Facebook Ads Manager 38
  Step 1: Creating Ad Campaign 38
    1. What is the Structure of Ads Manager? 38
    2. Ads Manager Guided and Quick Creation 41
  Step 2: Choosing Your Ad Campaign Goal 43

    2.1 Reach 43

    2.2 Post Engagement 44

    2.3 Page Likes 47

    2.4 Traffic 48

    2.5 Conversions 55

    2.6 Lead Generation 58

Step 3: Choosing Your Audience 60

    3.1 Targeting Options Overview 60

    3.1.1 Detailed Targeting 63

    3.1.2 Custom Audiences 64

    3.1.3 Lookalike Audiences 70

    3.2 How to Target Audience with High Income? 72

    3.3 Cold, Warm and Hot Audiences 73

    3.4 Excluding and Narrowing the Audience 75

    3.5 Placements and Devices 77

    3.6 Budgeting and Scheduling 83

Step 4: Creating an Effective Ad 87

    4.1 What Ad Formats are the Most Effective? 87

    4.2 How to Design a Good Ad Banner Easily? 95

    4.3 How to Write a Good Text 97

    4.4. What should You Know about Video Ads 98

Part III – Ad Nurturing Essentials 103

Chapter I – Everything You Need to Know about the Facebook Advertisement Mechanism 103

    1.   What is the Ad Delivery System and How is it Being Optimized? 103

    2.   What is the Learning Phase? 104

    3.   What is Auction and How does it Work? 104

Chapter 2 – How to Monitor an Ads' Performance Effectively 106

    2.1 What are the 4 Basic Metrics You Need to Monitor? 106

    2.2 How to Use Breakdowns? 111

Part IV – Troubleshooting Ad Performance **114**

Chapter I – Types of Performance Issues 114

    1.   Ads are not Spending Enough 114

    2.   Costs too High 115

Chapter 2 – Changes You can Make to Improve Performance..116

    2.1 Bid Strategy – Auction Issues 116

    2.2 Targeting – Audience Issues 118

    2.3 Creative – Ad Based Issues 119

    2.4 How to Chat with Support to Resolve any Issue 120

Conclusion **123**

List of Terms **130**

Introduction

Billions of people around the world spend their time on social media. This is the reason why businesses are embracing the concept of implementing advertisement strategies through these platforms. Facebook, being one of the most known social media platforms in the world, became a major part of the current digital marketing strategy. In fact, according to the 2018 Facebook Statistics, 2.32 billion people are using Facebook. This is why many entrepreneurs make advertisement on Facebook. One's ability to know how advertisement works in Facebook is an advantage especially in the business industry to ensure success and longevity.

This book is dedicated to all small business owners who want to better understand how to make small ad campaigns on Facebook by themselves. Also, this text will assist these owners who want to make more profit by using Facebook advertisements. Being an entrepreneur that is on trend with goods such as food & clothing or in services such as haircuts & health care can face a major challenge in marketing. In fact, this book will also benefit you in attracting potential customers for your business, by giving you fundamental knowledge of Facebook advertisement and how it works.

This book will give you a thorough understanding of the basics that you need to know first when creating an advertisement: How to create and setup an Ad account, choosing the right audience for your ads, and how to create different Ad formats. Moreover, tips on operating the ads effectively for your business will also be covered in this book. This tour guide will assist when you are creating your own advertisement. However, the book will not cover several topics that are too complex within this limited scope. Since some of the settings on creating advertisements are too complicated, the book will only feature the easiest and fastest way of learning how to create Facebook Ads.

At the end of reading this book, you will be able to understand how various advertisements work in the Facebook platform. You will also gain knowledge on using Facebook Business Manager and other important tools for your advertisements. Finally, you will also be able to create your own advertisements for your business not only on Facebook but also in Instagram as well.

Alexander Litavsky has been a prominent Facebook Advertising Specialist since 2014. He was a former lawyer but decided to follow his immense passion for Facebook advertising. Aside from his love for this field, he also plays piano, practices yoga, and engages in meditation. The dedication for his Facebook Advertising prowess resulted in more than $250,000 income for his clients' Ad Accounts. Alexander specializes in educational online businesses and offline events (particularly conferences) and lead generation. He creates advertisements for small and medium businesses like online photo, fast reading, and yoga schools. Additionally, he also provides traffic for offline conferences with 1000+ participants.

Alex also provides personal and group advertisement learning both online and offline available for his students. He writes articles and books with regards to Facebook advertisement. Alex also has his own Youtube Channel with free educational videos about Facebook advertisement. In turn, the author will help you to take a deeper look into the world of Facebook Advertisement.

For more information about the author, you can follow him on: ***https://www.facebook.com/lytavsky***

Part I Before the Beginning

Chapter I – Understanding Facebook Business Manager

1.1 What Is It and Why Do We Need It?

We all know that Facebook is one of the famous platforms used by advertisers for brand awareness. Televisions, radio, and other mediums are usually employed by large companies to inform people about their products. The only problem in these platforms is that it needs a couple, or even a large number, of people to advertise the product alone. For example, when creating a television advertisement, you need people from different departments to brainstorm and execute the advertisement. For small to intermediate entrepreneurs and with all the manpower and the costs, television advertisement is a bit too much to do right?

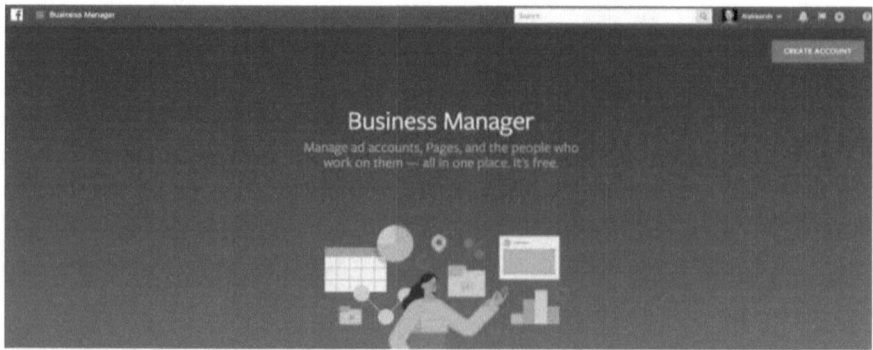

Figure 1: Business Manager

One good thing about advertising your products through Facebook is that you don't need a large number of people to advertise your product. You can do it with few people around you or if you want, you can do it on your own! Thanks to Facebook, there is a tool called ***Business Manager.*** This tool helps you to manage your ad accounts, pages, and access for people you work with for FREE. Moreover, the Business Manager makes it easy to control your business by serving as a personal organizer as it separates your business account from your personal account on Facebook.

It serves as a tracker for everything you do for your marketing and advertising. Some businesses prefer to work with a team for their social media marketing style, and this tool will also help them to manage the people they work with by assigning their designated roles for the ads and pages. Although Facebook is highly recommended this for businesses working with 1 or more employees, it can also be managed by a single person alone, especially if he/she wants to be organized and hands-on in his/her own business.

However, you can also choose not to use this tool if you are uncomfortable using this for advertisement purposes, as you can also make an advertisement using Boost Posts, which will be explained later.

One must remember that Business Manager is much needed when you are working as a team for your business, due to the fact that Business Manager allows you to control the access and permissions of the members for the business operations. Another reason why Business Manager is a helpful tool is that it adds security in your business with its safety features to ensure that your business information is thoroughly protected. Lastly, it is important to remember that you need the Business Manager if you want your business to grow. To make the things easier for you, a step by step tutorial on creating an account in *Business Manager* will be provided.

1.2 How to Create a Business Manager Account

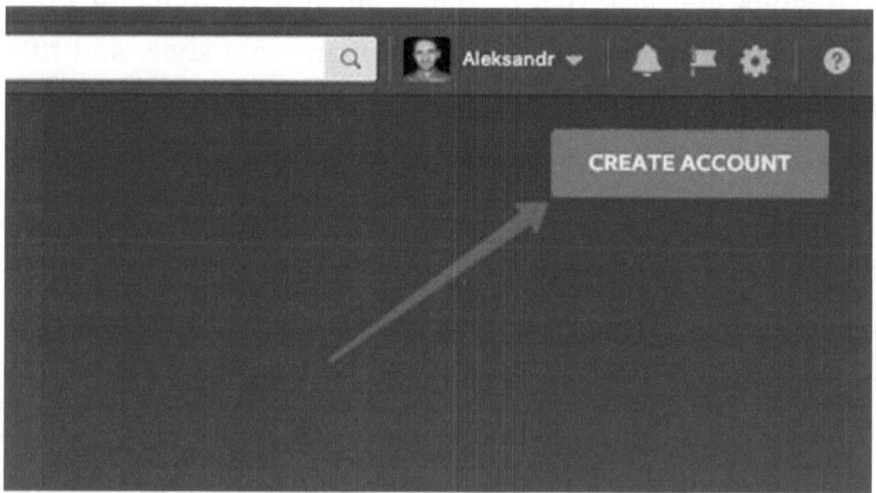

Figure 2: Create Account on Business Manager

To start creating your account, **go to the Business Manager webpage at <u>https://business.facebook.com/overview</u>.** On the top right side of the screen, select the button: "Create an Account." As seen on the picture, create your account in Business Manager by inserting your Business Name, your Name and your Business Email. Note that you must not put your personal email as your business email in order to separate your business account and personal account on Facebook. Then, supply all the necessary business details, which can be seen on the above picture on the right, to successfully create your Business Manager Account.

After creating an account, it will lead you to the Business Manager home panel:

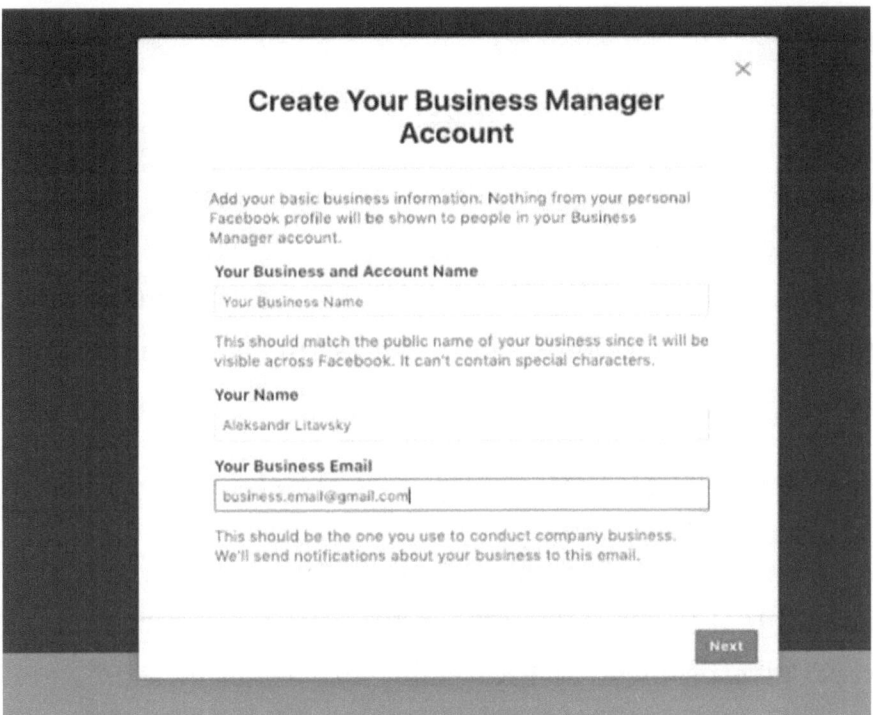

Figure 3: Business Manager Creation

The picture shown gives you a glimpse of which settings you can use in Business Manager. As you click the button on the left, shown with the red circle on the picture, you will find all the activities that you can do related to your business.

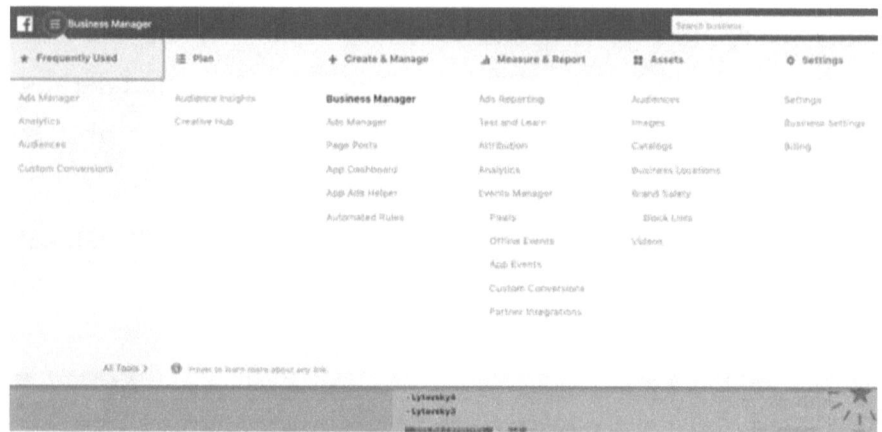

Figure 4: Business Manager Panel

From the planning stage, creating and managing it, as well as the reports for the business and the assets, everything can all be managed from this tab. To make this easier to understand, functions of the different settings to help build your advertisements on Business Manager will be discussed.

1.3 What is the Structure of Business Manager?

As mentioned earlier, the Facebook Business Manager is a helpful tool that serves as a tracker on whatever you do for your advertisement in Facebook. This works by letting you add users in your Ad Account and handle the different features on Facebook. To have a further understanding of its structure. You may refer to the diagram given below.

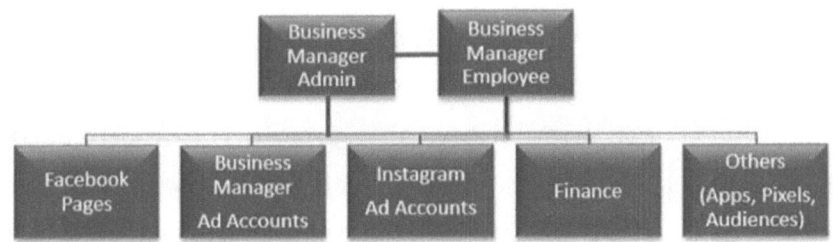

Figure 4: Business Manager Structure

The basic structure of Business Manager is evident in the diagram. Through the Admin that created the Ad Account, he/she may add employees or people who will help him/her to manage the other Facebook features. Hence, the admin can also assign roles to the other co-handler of the account on what features they can access in Facebook. If the admin wants the user to only have access to the Finance features, that is the only feature that the user can access. These roles will be further elaborated on the next lessons.

The features of Business Manager are vast. Thus, you must be aware of its structure such as: *Administration of User Roles, Account Access and Ad Account Finances, Asset Sharing among your team, Product Catalog Creation, Metrics about your advertisements* and *Publishing of your Ads*. Some of these features will not be discussed in this book due to their complexity. However, we will still mention the basic features essential for creating an advertisement.

It is also important to remember that there are also legal reasons why we recommend you to have a Facebook Business Manager. One reason is the implementation of the European Union's GDPR or General Data Protection Regulation. This rule allows companies to have a legal claim of all their Facebook Data. Thus, all assets under the company's Ad Account will also be added to the company's legal structure of ownership. These stipulations also denote the main reason why Facebook is recommending you not to use a personal account in creating the business manager. Since this tool is structured for business, once a person leaves the company and his or her Facebook account is used for the Business Manager, you may lose an access to the ad account. Unlike if you are using a business account for this purpose, your business has the full legal ownership of all the Ads and Pages that you have created. Another rationale for separating your personal life to your professional life is that, Facebook Business Manager is structured in a way that you don't have to receive notifications about your business' Pages and Ads all the time on your personal Facebook Account since you have a different profile for your business through Business Manager. In terms of security structure, since Business Manager is separated to your personal Facebook account, so you can still access your Business Manager account even if your personal account is hacked.

Now that you have a general understanding of the internal structure of Business Manager, let us now go to the external structure of Business Manager. The features that will be discussed are those that are most integral and most commonly used for your advertisements.

Settings

The settings page is where you can see all information with regards to your Business Manager account. In fact, it is where you can also preview the assigned assets to the users added in your Business Manager account. Any information related to your pages, data sources and security can be observed in this setting. It actually summarizes the entirety of Business Manager as it gives you general information of every detail that you input into the account.

If you click the settings, your Ad Account Setup will appear. This step will give you the information about your account ID and the currency you are using for billing of your advertisements.

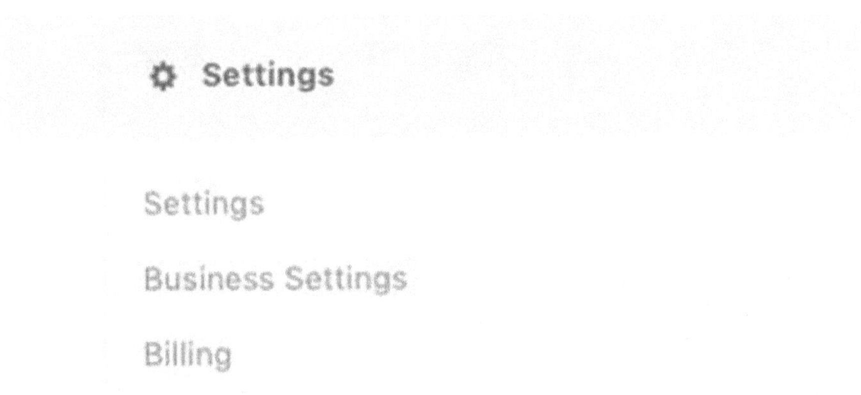

☼ Settings

Settings

Business Settings

Billing

Figure 5: Settings

Create & Manage

Create & Manage allows you to add Pages, add Ad Accounts and add People to the Business Manager. Just by clicking the Add People, you may enter the username of your co-workers and assign their roles for the project. Also, Clicking Add Pages and Ad Accounts may be used to merge your existing pages and ad accounts to the Business Manager or used to create a new one.

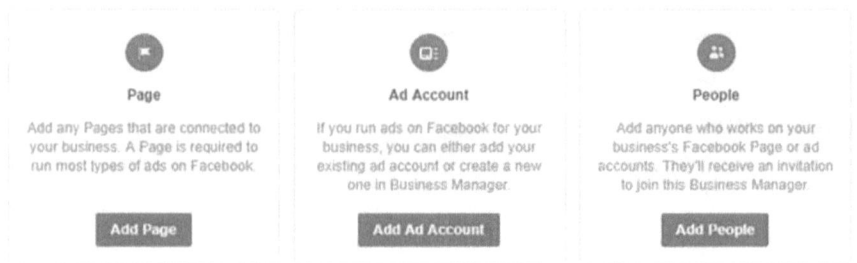

Figure 6: Create & Manage

Under the Create & Manage page, there are several Ad and App managing tools that you can use to monitor your Ad Activities. Starting with the **Ads Manager.** Ads Manager is one of the essential tools for creating an advertisement in the Facebook Business Manager. It is where you can devise and assign objective campaigns, choose the audience and placement of the Ad, and assign the budget for your advertisement. This will be elaborated further later.

Page Posts, on the other hand, will let you monitor your business pages and see the advertisements that you posted. Using this tool will also enable you to view how many audiences your advertisements reached and how many clicks you managed to have while using those advertisements. Thus, it will help you to determine which advertisement is the most effective among the audience.

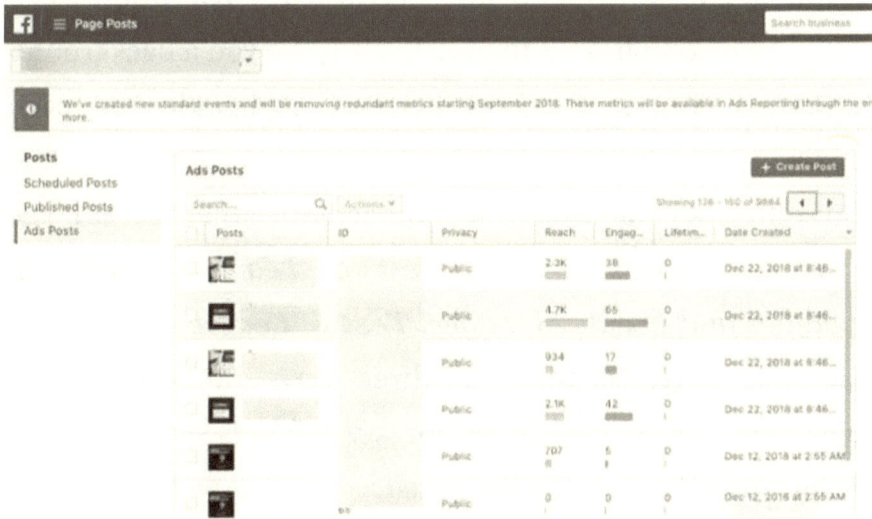

Figure 7: Page Posts

Meanwhile, if you're an App developer who wants to enhance its advertisements, the ***App Dashboard & App Ads Helper*** is perfect for you! This platform will help you to check your app settings as well as the activity on your application advertisements.

Measure & Report

This setting in Business Manager allows you to create reports using the performance data available from your advertisements. This feature will also help you analyze and explore what advertisements have potential in reaching larger audiences. You can also create and share reports to your co-workers or even stakeholders.

However, **the setting is not mandatory for beginners** as it is a bit complicated to use. Just to give you a background on how it works, here's a detailed explanation of each activity.

The setting is composed of several activities that you can use to create reports namely: *Test & Learn, Attribution, Analytics and Events Manager.* **Test & Learn** assist you to test your advertisements in three ways by choosing its questions. You may set it up for 5-7 minutes depending on the question that you have selected.

The tests must run with the minimum amount of 7 days and the setup time to give all the information it needed is also provided. Facebook also gives a description of every test that they added in Business Manager to guide advertisers when utilizing this tool. You may also cancel the test anytime if you feel like you don't need it anymore by clicking the Learn Panel and selecting "Cancel Test" to your test.

Attribution, on the other hand, is used to choose the line of organization for your business. You may select if your business is a Single business, Multiple businesses with separate brands, or Agency. You may use Attribution to see only relevant data for each brand that you have in your business. However, you may skip this setting if you find it difficult for you to set it up, especially if you don't have several lines of business.

Additionally, a setting in Measure & Report that should be remembered is the **Analytics,** which refers to where all the data collected are stored from the beginning of your Ad creation to your current Ad activities on Facebook. If you're familiar with Google Analytics, Facebook Analytics also works the same way. However, the difference of Facebook Analytics is that it can see the activities including the Active Users and Audience Impact on your advertisements in a smaller and more personal scale. Google Analytics, on the other hand, covers a large scale of collecting advertising data. Google Analytics and Facebook Analytics also have difference in using tracking tools. Google Analytics uses *Cookie Tracking* in order to track the actions of the users. Cooking Tracking means that the actions of a user are stored in the browser and the information can be accessed by the server. Meanwhile, Facebook Analytics uses *User Tracking* that knows its users through their own profile. It is better than the Cookie Tracking because Facebook can track the Ads that the user clicked, as well as the purchases and views that the user made in the past 24 hours!

Lastly, **Events Manager** is where you can see the *Facebook Pixel, Offline Events and App Events.* It serves as a simplified tool for managing your monitoring for your advertising activities. *Offline Events* is an advantage for businesses that are sales-driven, since it is more focuses on purchasing, bookings and other sales related activities. *App Events*, on the other hand, functions as a measuring tool for app developers as they can monitor the activities of audiences who use the app.

1.4 What Roles Are There?: The Difference Between Partners and People

Some people tend to not recognize the difference between partners and people in Business Manager. However, there is a huge difference between the two. Facebook **Business Partners** are those users from other businesses who you work with such as Ad agencies for your business. If you want a business/agency to give permission to view or edit your assets in Business Manager, you can add them to your account. To add a partner in your Business Manager, you must remember to be an admin of the account, and the partner should also have a Business Manager account. This designation is due to the fact that you need the Business ID of your partner to add him or her to your account.

The steps needed to add partners/agencies to your business involves going to the Business Settings and under the **Users** tab, select **Partners.** Then, select the **+Add** button. You will be required to enter the *Partner Business ID*. If your partner can't find his or her ID, he or she may go to the Business Settings and select the Business Info tab to give you the Business ID. After entering the Partner Business ID, you may select the assets that you would like the partner to have an access with including one's roles to your account.

Meanwhile, **People** are individual people with whom you work with for your business. You may add people to the business manager by entering their email addresses. You must remember that those people that you will add will receive an email about your user request. The only time that they will be added to your account is when they accept your request.

To add people to your account, go to the Business Settings and click **People.** Select the **+Add** button then enter the email addresses of the people you want to add to the account. Then, select the role you would like them to have. The roles will be further discussed in the following chapters. Lastly, select **Add People** to send an email request.

1.5 How to Add an Existing Ad Account to Business Manager

Ad Account is really important when creating an advertisement whether you use the Facebook Business Manager or not. As you create an advertisement on

Facebook, you are automatically creating an Ad account. You must remember that you can't proceed with the creation of your Ads without setting up an Ad Account. So, if you're curious on what an Ad Account is and what it does, here is a guide on how you will do it:

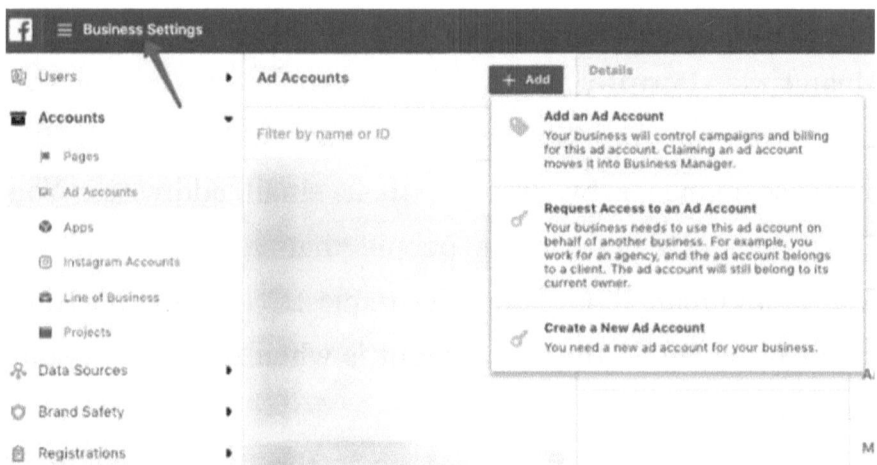

Figure 8: Ad Account

As you have seen in the last chapter of the Facebook Business Manager walk-through, you can add an Ad Account by using the Settings tab and selecting the Ad Accounts on the left panel. If you don't have any Ad Accounts yet, you'll be able to see the Add button in the screen as seen on the picture on the right. By clicking it, you will be given three options:

Add an Ad Account – This option lets you create an additional Ad account to your existing account in Business Manager

Request Access to an Ad Account – This setting is used if you're not the Admin of the Ad account and would like to request access to it. It is also the right option if you need to utilize an Ad account on behalf of another business.

Create a New Ad Account – This last option enables you to create a new Ad account if you currently don't have any Ad account for your business.

For beginners, it is better to choose the third option which is the creation of a New Ad Account since you don't have any Accounts yet. New Ad Account option will allow you to choose what country you're in and also the currency you want to use for your billing methods.

You must remember that all businesses who wants to create a business manager are only able to create 1 Ad account. However, you can host a maximum of 5 Ad accounts if you have an active spend to your current account. To be able to add an existing account in Business Manager, you may choose the first option which is the *Add an Ad Account*. By selecting this option, an Ad account will be moved permanently to your Business Manager. Remember that you are not able to add an Ad account that is owned by another business. If you want to do so, you may request an access to an Ad account by clicking the second option. Thus, the admin of the Ad account must give you permission to work for the existing Ad account. For easier access of adding ad accounts, you must be the owner/admin of the Ad account and also the Business Manager.

Facebook Business Manager is a very powerful tool in marketing, and it plays an eminent role in organizing and monitoring your advertisements on Facebook. This section showed the most important aspects to remember when using Facebook Business Manager such as: payments, time zones, and roles. We also saw how advanced technology is being used to monitor advertising activities and the influences it can make to reach other people. Thus, let us maximize the usage of this tool by creating innovative ideas to encourage and positively influence people. Always remember that you are not just a simple entrepreneur, but you can also be an influencer in advocating for the betterment of the world!

Chapter 2 – How to Correctly Setup an Ad Account

2.1 Payment Methods

You can also click the Payment setting to be informed of when your next bill is. One important facet to remember in the Settings tab is that it is where you can find the **Payment methods** for your Ad accounts.

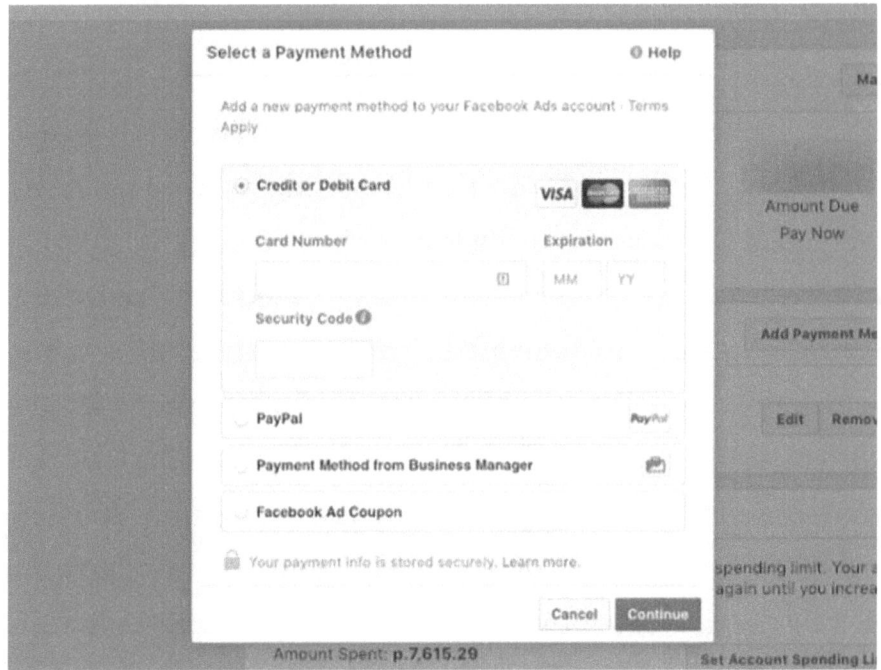

Figure 9: Select Payment Method

The picture shows how you can select your payment method for your Ad accounts depending on your country. The usual method for paying is Credit Card or Debit Card.

You may also remove a payment method from your Ad Account by using the Facebook Business Manager and access it through its Settings. Removing your primary payment method means that you don't want to use it anymore to pay for your ads. Be sure that you're the admin of the ad account, so you'll have an access to the billing methods.

If you're working as a team, you can also request for an account permission if you don't have access to the ad account. However, it is better if the admin of the ad account does the removal of the payment method to lessen the hassle of doing it.

If you just want to remove the payment method and change it to another, you can still do this by adding another payment method first before removing the original account.

In terms of your concern with billing, **Account Spending Limit** is a term to remember. In fact, setting an account spending limit will control your total ad costs. Your ads will automatically pause once you reach the limit you have set for your ads unless you increase or remove the limit. You can create an account spending limit by going to the Payment Settings and clicking the *Account Spending Limit* option in the Set tab.

Another way of a billing method is the **Billing Threshold**. It serves as the same way like Account Spending Limit but differs as far as its functions. Billing Threshold works when you run your ads and accumulate an ad cost. It will start on an amount based on your chosen country and currency for your Ad account. Facebook will automatically charge you if the amount you spend reaches the Billing Threshold you have set. Hence, you will receive a bill once you reach your billing threshold for a given month.

2.2 Currency

As mentioned formerly, you are required to choose your currency during the creation of your Ad account. Your payment methods will depend on the currency that you will choose. These criteria are due to the fact that some payment methods are still not available in a country. You must also remember that if you're living in a country like Brazil, Venezuela and Nigeria, it must match its business country and currency. The reason of this is that, Facebook follows certain foreign exchange regulations in those countries. Facebook released a list of accepted currencies that may help you for the Facebook Ads billing.

2.3 Timezone: Why is it Important?

Keep in mind that it is important not only to setup your payment account but also to set the appropriate time zone. **Timezone** is the specific area or region that follows a certain time. You may change your time zone by clicking the *Change Timezone* button during the Ad Account Setup.

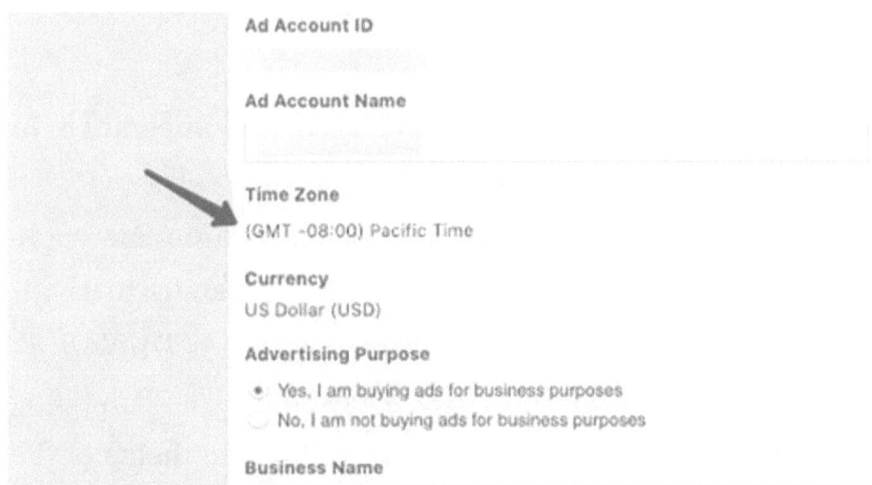

Figure 10: Change Time Zone

Every time you create new ad accounts, notice that the default time zones are in PST (Pacific Standard Time), so be sure to change it to your corresponding time zone or else your existing account will be deactivated, and your ads will stop running if you change it after you already created an ad account.

Account setup may seem to be simple at first sight. However, you must remember to be responsible in every action that you take especially because it requires your money in placing an advertisement. Verify that you know what you are getting into is very important, especially that you are risking your time, money, and opportunity in doing Facebook Advertisements. If you're having a problem with your Ad accounts, you may visit the Facebook Business | Ads Help Center to give you more insights about your account.

Chapter 3 – What is a Key to Success in Facebook Advertising?

3.1 Setting Your Goals

Goals or objectives for your business are imperative in creating advertising campaigns. In fact, they will serve as a steering wheel in your whole advertising path on Facebook. Advertising campaigns must be **SMART**. Meaning to say, it must be *SPECIFIC, MEASURABLE, ATTAINABLE, REALISTIC and TIME-BOUND*. Questions like "How long should this campaign be?" or "What will be the theme of the campaign?" can help you to determine your goals for advertising your business. To guide you in making your goals, always remember what things you want to prioritize when campaigning for your business. **Create a list** of your vision for your business and turn it into goals. For example, if you want people to be aware of your business, then make it as your first priority to create a brand awareness. In fact, it's easier to reach out to people who are close to you. This demographic can be group of people whom you know or those people who live near your business. Let them be your target audience as you create your first advertisement. Then, you can start to "Boost" your post to reach larger audience. This concept will be further explained in the next lessons.

3.2 Working with Strategy: Facebook Ads Funnel

As noted, technology has been advancing as time passes. Not only people are coping with it, but they are also coping with all the environmental aspects that revolve around it, including business. This reason reflects why businesses are making their way through digital marketing. ***Digital Marketing Strategy*** is used to support the usual marketing strategy of a business by means of technology. Through the use of various social media platforms, businesses can penetrate the market effectively. Thus, Facebook Ads is only a part of the Digital Marketing Strategy that we can use to attract potential customers to our business. Of course, we can use it to increase sales. One common challenge that a business may face in creating digital marketing strategy is the strategy itself.

A strategy known as **Facebook Funnel** is extremely helpful to keep your potential customers on track. By funneling, your strategy is to transform the cold audience to warm audience. This strategy means that you are transforming their desire to purchase your product. Once they follow the funnel path, you are expecting them to buy your products and generate more sales. This strategy actually plays an important role in getting higher rates of visitors and sales. It's a strategy that will start first from having a broad target audience to smaller scale of people, just like a funnel.

Funneling is much recommended if you have a Facebook Pixel. The guide for Facebook Pixel will be discussed on the next lessons. Make sure to list all the URLs from your website that you want to use as a Funnel in your Facebook Ads Manager. The URLs can be a homepage or certain parts of your website that you want the visitors to be directed to. URLs will also serve as the navigation path for your website visitors later on. As you create your Ads in the Ads Manager, select the Create Audience button then Custom Audience. By clicking the Website Traffic option, you can input all the URLs you have chosen from your website. Verify that you select the Create Audience after inputting all the URLs to save your work.

To make it easier for you to do, here's a basic look of a Facebook Funnel:

Stage 1: *Creating an Ad for Brand Awareness.* Creating an Ad that increases audience awareness will help you to attract customers who are still unaware of your product. The broader the audience, the better for this stage.

Stage 2: *Using Custom Audience for your Ads to target potential customers.* This stage allows you to focus on users who will most likely buy your product.

Stage 3: *Building customer relationships.* This stage enables you to persuade users that they need your product. Creating Ads and answering all comments on the Ads are relevant in this stage. Building relationships to your potential customers can likely increase the chance of them actually buying your product.

Stage 4: *Making the users take an action.* Using Ads that allow users take an action such as "Shop Now" Ads are vital in this stage.

Stage 5: *Audience Purchasing.* By this stage, people should already be purchasing your product. Monitor the results through Facebook Business Manager to see how many visitors have purchased your product.

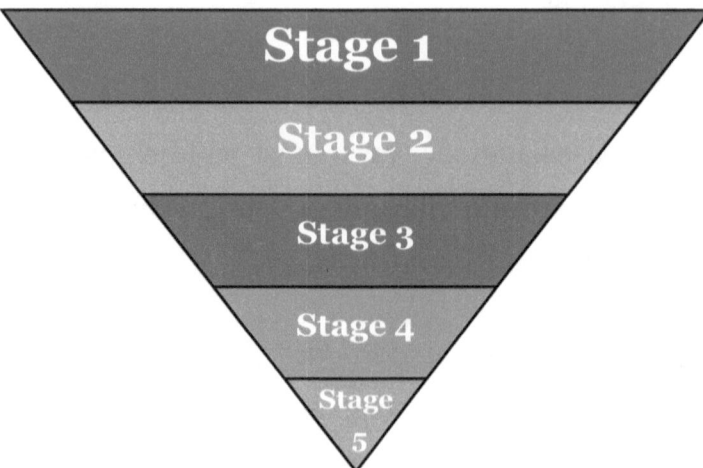

Figure 11: Facebook Funnel

As you can see, it started from a broader scale until it slowly turned into a smaller scale. This trend represents the stages where people are being filtered as time goes by until they purchase your product.

You can monitor the results of the data in Facebook Business Manager Audience Section. The results could take from hours up to days depending on how many visitors you have for your website. There are times that even if you use funnel, some audiences are still not encouraged to buy your product. To avoid wasting money for your advertisements, analyze the mistakes you have made that drawn the audience not to buy your product. Factors like less interaction or wrong audience targeting may contribute to some potential mistakes. The URLs you provided in the Custom Audience section also serve an important role. These URLs will drive the audience directly to a part of your website where you want them to purchase. So, double-check to analyze which stage you need to improve in funneling.

3.3 Knowing Your Target Audience

Thanks to the brilliant minds of people behind Facebook, advertising gets easier as they help you to target the audience that you care about for your business. If you remember correctly, using the Ads Manager in Facebook Business Manager can help you to target audience via the Ad Set settings during the creation of the Ad. In business, there's a term called *Buyer Persona,* which is used by businesses to know their target audience. This term is a somehow fictional representation of the profile of your target customers. This notion usually includes demographics of the people you are targeting. Characteristics like interests, location, gender and age are pivotal in thinking about your target audience. It is better if you think of more detailed characteristics to help you to focus exclusively for your advertisements. Other characteristics like language and connections are essential.

Use your buyer personas to incorporate the characteristics as you create your Facebook advertisements. You may do so during the Ad Set creation in the Ads Manager and selecting the Audience for your advertisement. This process will be further discussed in the next few lessons.

3.4 Effectively Using Target Instruments

Creating an advertisement on Facebook may seem initially overwhelming. In fact, when you are using Business Manager, there are many options to choose to target your audience. The question is, how sure are you that you are using these instruments effectively?

One factor that we want to avoid when creating Ads is spending too much on the wrong areas of advertising. This reason reflects why targeting instruments are made: to ensure that you are on the right track of advertising your business. Several tips can help you to effectively target your audience:

- **Be creative to attract visitors.** As stated earlier, brand awareness is important to make people know your product. Actually, if you really want to create brand awareness, you may do so by selecting it as an objective on your Ad and using boosted posts.
- **Selecting the right audience.** During the Ad Set creation, which will be discussed later, validate that you have selected the right audience preference for your Ads. In fact, this step is very critical for your Ads' effectiveness. If you are following the Facebook Funneling Strategy, it is recommended to choose broader audience at first and then lessen as time passes. Make sure to frequently adjust the audience to ensure that your Ads are still applicable as time elapses.

- **Use Lead Generation.** You may use several promotions such as discounts and freebies for your target customers to attract them more. This objective will not only build the relationship with your targets, but it can also bring them closer into buying your product. Another benefit is that you can have an access with their information as they give you their contacts. This topic will be further discussed in the next lessons.
- **Increase Promotions.** This strategy may not only be done by you but your customers as well. As those people from your leads became your customers, you may encourage them to promote your product by several ways. People may promote your product by sharing the current promotions you have and tagging their friends in Facebook. Thus, it will gradually attract more target customers over time.

Choosing an Audience actually plays a large role in advertising. They are the ones who will determine the effectivity of your advertisements. Knowing who you will target and how many people you are planning to reach is eminent as you create your advertisements. Always remember your objective and this is to attract them and let them buy your product. As long as you're in line with your goals and objectives, you will not be lost in your advertising path on Facebook.

Part II – 4 Steps to Create Advertisement in Facebook Ads Manager

Step 1: Creating Ad Campaign

1. What is the Structure of Ads Manager?

If you remember correctly the concepts and tips discussed in the Facebook Business Manager, Facebook Ads Manager is a place where you can create and assign objective campaigns, choose the audience and placement of the Ad, and assign the budget for your advertisement. It is a more advanced tool of advertising since you can customize the Facebook Ads through the Ads manager. Facebook Ads created in Ads Manager are more specific in its business goals. Facebook Ads allows you to choose different ad placements and maintain a creative control as your design fits your objectives for your advertising campaign.

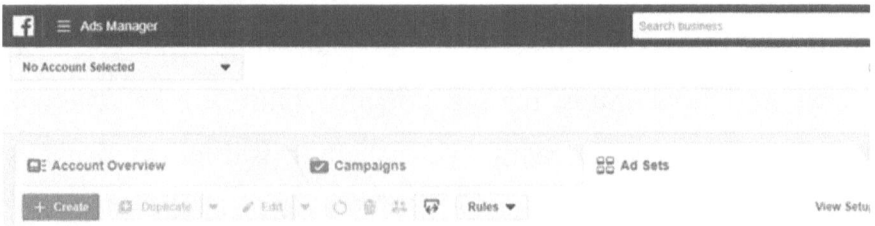

Figure 12: Ads Manager

Under the Ads Manager, you can see in the left panel the *Campaign, Ad Set and Ad tabs*. The **Campaign** tab allows you to select an objective for your business. You may create an Ad Campaign under the Ads Manager. By clicking the Create Button, a left side panel will appear.

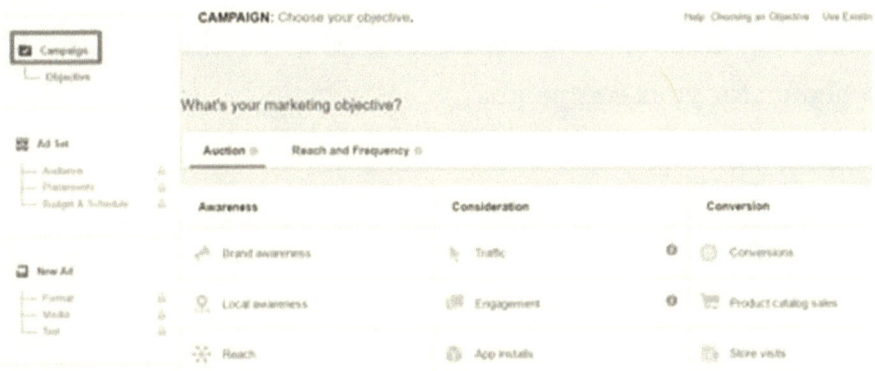

Figure 13: Campaign Creation

Choose the campaign on the left side panel. Then, click your desired objective that you want to be seen in your Ad. You can only choose one objective for your advertisement. However, you must remember that you already have an Ad account to be able to use create an Ad campaign.

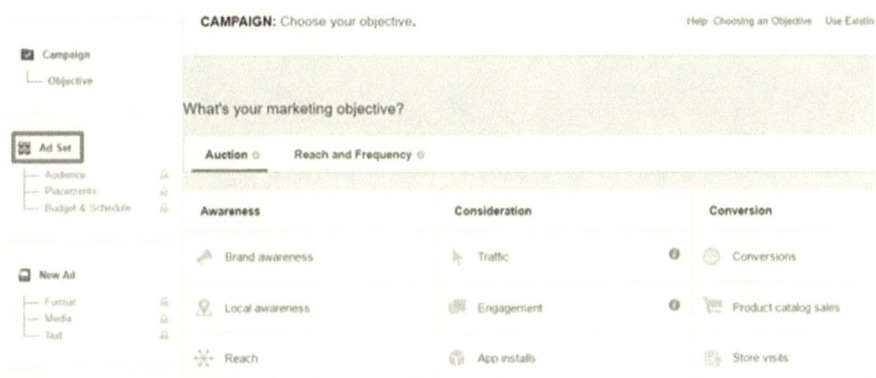

Figure 14A: Ad Set Creation

By using Ads Manager in creating your campaigns, it will also require you to have an Ad Set before you proceed with the confirmation of your Ads. ***Ad Set*** is where you will tell how your Ad will run. In essence, this place denotes where you will assign the page (if you have multiple pages for your business), audience, placement, as well as the budgets & schedule for your campaign.

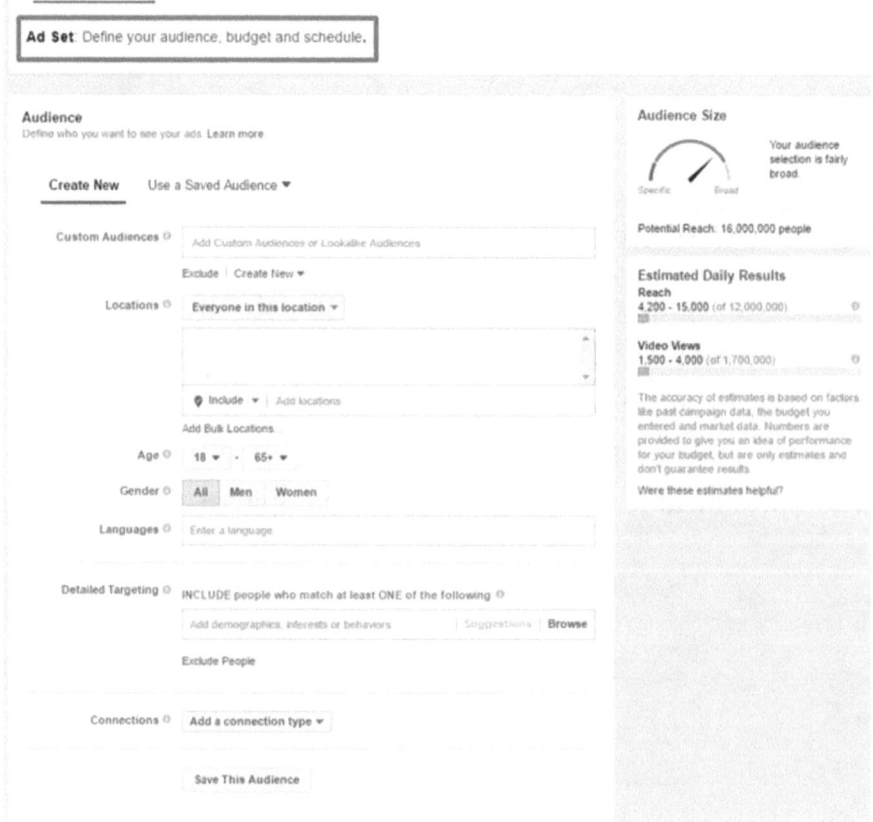

Figure 14B: Ad Set Creation

Again, your currency in placing the budget depends on how you formerly set up your Ad account, so you must have placed the currency and country you're in before you proceed with the Ad Set. Ad Set will also provide you with estimated reach of your ads as it measures the data you have input from your campaign, budget, and audience.

After setting up everything, you may proceed with the creation of your advertisement which will be under the **Ad** tab.

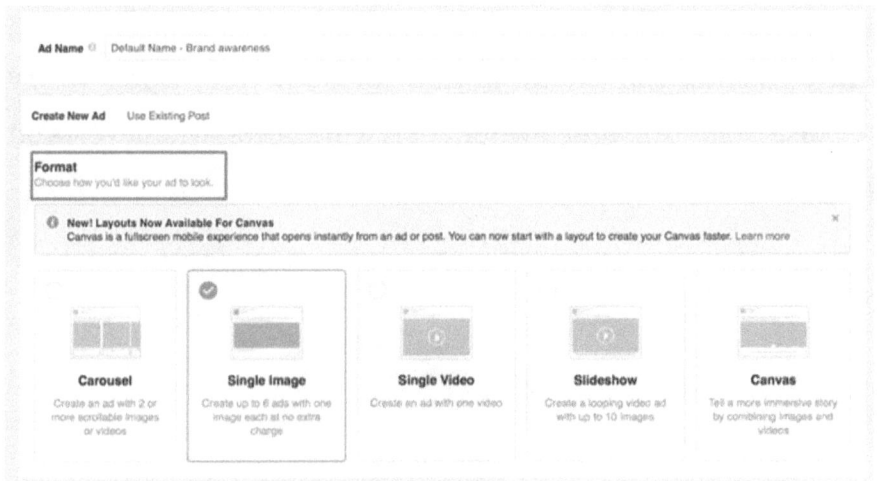

Figure 15: Ad Format

The Ad tab includes the selecting for the Format of your ad, the media that you are going to use, and other additional creatives that you would like to include in your advertisements. Lastly, selecting the confirm button will create all the chosen settings for your ad.

2. Ads Manager Guided and Quick Creation

There are two ways for creating an ad in Ads Manager: **Guided Creation** or **Quick Creation.** Guided Creation helps you by giving several steps to use when launching your basic campaigns. This option is recommended for users who are new to Facebook Ads and want to be guided step by step in creating their own advertisements. Meanwhile, Quick Creation is an option to make a Campaign, Ad Set and Ad. This workflow is recommended for people who are already familiar with Facebook Ads. As you choose which workflow you prefer, it will automatically become your default setting when clicking the Create button for your Ads. Don't worry because you can still switch the workflows whenever you want.

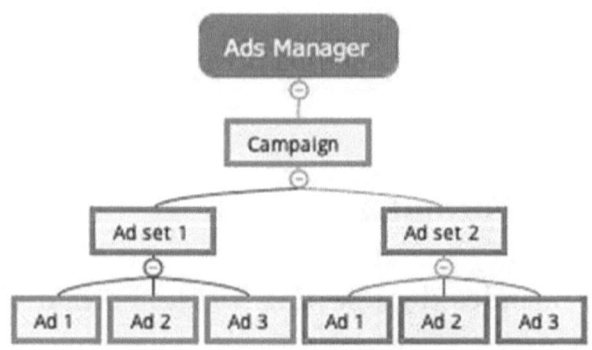

Figure 16: Sample workflow

The picture above is an example of a workflow for Guided and Quick Creation. As you can see, the structure of Ads Manager is shown through a process which started from a Campaign until the Ad is created.

In terms of publishing your Ads, both options have different functions. In Guided Creation, your campaign will publish automatically as you click the confirm button. Guided Creation is easier to use since you don't need to review your ads and Facebook is guiding you along the way. However, in Quick creation, you have to save everything as a draft. You may edit the Campaign, Ad Set and Ad in any orders any time you want before you publish it.

Step 2: Choosing Your Ad Campaign Goal

2.1 Reach

When choosing your Ad Campaign Goal, the first objective that you need to know is the **Reach Objective.** This type of objective helps you to boost the numbers of viewers who see your advertisements. Use this type of objective if you want to create brand awareness for your business so you can monitor how often people see your Ads. You may choose this objective during the Ad Campaign creation. Thus, this will lead you to the Ad Set setting. If you click the "Show more options" at the bottom of the Budget section, you can see several options for your ads. Setting the *Frequency Cap* can also help you to successfully use this kind of objective. Frequency cap is a way of keeping other people seeing your Ads too often. Capping can be done by adjusting the number of times the person will see your Ad in a given period of time. It is recommended to lower the frequency cap for 1-2 Ads per week to avoid overexposure of your Ads.

During the ad creation, you can observe that there are about the Potential Reach and Estimated Daily Reach. *Potential Reach* is the estimated number of people connected through your ads. It offers merely an idea of how many people and how wide your advertisement can reach. *Estimated Daily Reach* is a more precise number as it gives you an idea of how many people are targeted each day. However, both of these are just representation of your campaign and is not an exact number of people reached. Estimates sometimes do not match your data and may show gaps when monitored. The numbers are there just to help your advertisement's effectiveness. Don't worry because Facebook still uses tools and factors such as performance of other advertisers to make it more accurate as much as possible. Every time that you adjust the budget on the Ad set, the number of reach also moves. This mechanism is just a way for Facebook to tell you how many people can be reached if you use a certain amount of budget for your advertisement. It still depends on how many people you want to reach for your particular business.

2.2 Post Engagement

Post Engagement is used to increase page posts attraction. You can use Post Engagement through your Page posts and let people take action by clicking your advertisement. it is used to see the people who are most likely interested to your Ads. The specialty of post engagement is a metric that lets you compare the engagement of the people from other ads or campaign.

Post Engagement most likely works with Ads Manager unlike **Boosted Posts** that can be accessed through your Facebook page alone. Boosted Posts are simpler way of advertising. You can boost a post through your Facebook Page. However, it only optimizes items in your posts such as the likes, comments and shares unlike with Facebook Ads, where you can control several ad objectives for your campaign. Using boosted posts will make you choose whether you want to place your Ad on Instagram in addition to what you currently have on Facebook Mobile and the Desktop News Feed. It is important if you know the exact goals of your business, so you can choose whether you are going to use boosted posts or create an Ad using the Ads Manager, so you can maximize your Ad campaigns. Actually, if you really want to create brand awareness, using boosted posts is definitely for you!

The picture shows a sample of where you can find the "Boost post" button. It can be seen in any posts that you've made on the Facebook page of your business. By selecting it, you will see a dialogue box that will let you adjust the budget for the boosting. The default setting is $20 but the minimum budget that you can put is $1 per day. Boosted posts have several features that can give you more advantage in advertising.

Several of these features include: Defining new audiences based on their location, interests and etc., more Ad placements on Desktop NewsFeed, Mobile NewsFeed & Instagram and access to the results of your promotions on the Promotions tab of your Facebook page.

Both of Boosted Posts and Ads Manager Posts increase the engagement of likes, comments, and shares. The difference is just the broadness of the target options. In Ads Manager, you may be able to edit the target placement and audience for your business. It allows you to propose a bigger amount of target options, which we recommend you to use. Facebook Ads Manager is a place where you can create your Ads and be more specific in advertising your business.

The effectivity of the two types of Post Engagement may differ from person to person. Some people say that boosting post through page only wastes money. Some claim that creating an Ad is more efficient as it is more detailed than boosting a post. Others suggest that boosting posts create more clicks for their website from their experiences. You may try to use both if you want and monitor their diverse effectiveness afterwards. The most important tip is to drive people's interests in your business.

Figure 17: Boost Post

2.3 Page Likes

Page Likes is a term used to refer to how many likes your Facebook Page has gained from your advertisements. You can use this notion as a Campaign goal by choosing ***Engagement*** as your objective. This objective is most likely designed to let people see and be engaged on your Facebook Posts or Page. Through the Page Like Objective, you can make ads that can: *Boosts your posts, Promote your Page, Offer Claims* and *Increase Attendance for your Events.* Using this kind of objective for your Ads can help you in increasing your ad impressions. Also, as one of your objectives, it will make Facebook show the ads to the people who are most likely like to comment on and share your post.

The platforms that support this kind of objective include: Facebook, Instagram and Audience Network. Meanwhile, Ad formats that you can use in this objective are: Photo, Video, Carousel and Slideshow. Keep in mind that certain ad formats are only available for this objective.

There are certain ways to increase page likes for your business. First, you can use Call-To-Action advertisement that has a "like" button so an audience can like your page anytime. As long as you are posting a relevant content, this tactic would be effective to reach a larger audience.

Making your ads personal for the audience can also increase page likes. For example, if your business is about renting a venue, you may post an ad about a wedding picture of a customer who rented your place. By doing so, people relating to this post will have a better idea of what they can do with your business.

You must remember to monitor the ads performance through the Ads Manager regularly. Doing so will enable you to see how many likes and impressions your Ads have reached through this objective.

2.4 Traffic

In terms of considering your target audience, always remember your end goal, which is to make them buy your product. Your goal as you create your Ad campaigns should drive people to your pages, make them click, and buy your product. Facebook has a setting where you can create an Ad and put a traffic objective in your advertisement. We all know that when we use Facebook, we can see advertisements that have "Visit Website," "Learn More," "Shop Now," or "Book Now" button at the bottom of the Ads.

Figure 18: Traffic Ad Sample

This is an example of a **traffic objective.** This goal is largely used when there is not enough audience for a conversion goal, as it sends people to a destination on your website or page. It works when you create your ad in the Ads Manager and enables you to choose your objective before you proceed with the creation of the Ad.

Remember to use this goal if you want to increase the number of people by selecting where you want to drive the traffic in your page or your website. Platforms under the Facebook management supports traffic objective such as: *Facebook itself, Instagram, Messenger* and *Audience Network*. Keep in mind that there are only few ad formats that support the traffic objective, and these are: *Single image, Single Video, Carousel, Slideshow* and *Collection*.

Additionally, if you want to use this objective for your advertisements, you'll need to set up the **Facebook Pixel** for your website to monitor the traffic. Facebook Pixel is an analytics tool available in the Facebook Business Manager that allows a user to see the effectiveness of the advertising by analyzing the actions people visiting your website. Facebook Pixel is helpful to ensure that your advertisements are being shown to the right audience. Also, it is useful in building an advertising audience and unlocking additional Facebook advertising tools.

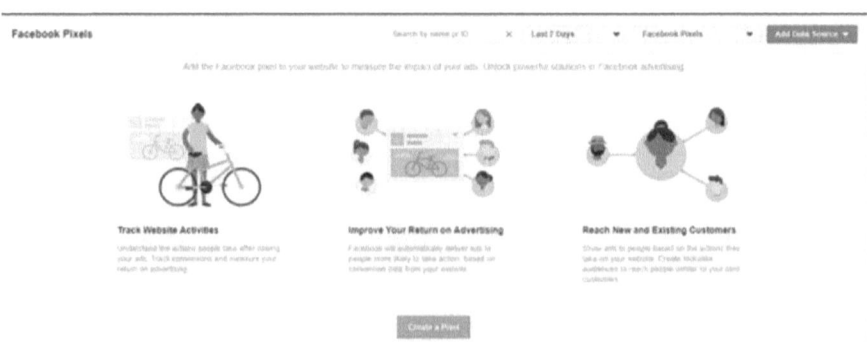

Figure 19: Facebook Pixel

Actually, we are recommending Facebook Pixel to businesses that have websites, since the main goal of Facebook Pixel is to place a pixel code on the header of your website to measure the visits and actions of audiences on your websites. By using Facebook Pixel, you can reach out to a customer again as he or she visits your website through the Facebook Ads you've posted. In fact, there are many benefits of using Facebook Pixel for your website. You can reach the right people specifically, as you can see who has visited your website. Thus, using Facebook Pixel can help you to create Lookalike Audiences to drive more people to your website. Of course, your main goal is to drive more sales; by using Facebook Pixel, you can set up automatic bidding to target people who are more likely buy from your website. By observing the information of your conversions and sales, you may estimate the results of your Ads. If you're wondering how you will install a pixel on your website, here's a guide on how you can do it.

You must remember that Facebook Pixel is only possible if you have a website for your business. Thus, you must also be knowledgeable in updating your website's codes. Create your Facebook Pixel account by accessing it in the Events Manager tab in the Facebook Business Manager. If you click the **Create Pixel** button, a pop-up dialogue box will appear. Once you've created the pixel on your website, you must add events to track specific actions people do in your website.

If you're wondering what *Events* mean, these are actions that happen on your website. For example, if a customer books or purchases on your website and you input a code on your website, it will help you to track an event and also help Facebook to understand that someone took an action on your website. In fact, Facebook is recommending users to install the code manually by choosing "**Manually Install the Code yourself**" during the setup of Pixels, so that you can edit the events to track your website. However, it is recommended to put the code in the header section of your website, not in the body, so there will still be a pixel count even if the page didn't reload properly. If you put it in the body section, the pixel won't be counted if a visitor closed the browser or if it didn't load properly. Additionally, you can install the events by clicking the "**Install Events**" button. The details and information you want to track on your website can be chosen such as: Contact, Location, Add to Cart, and many more.

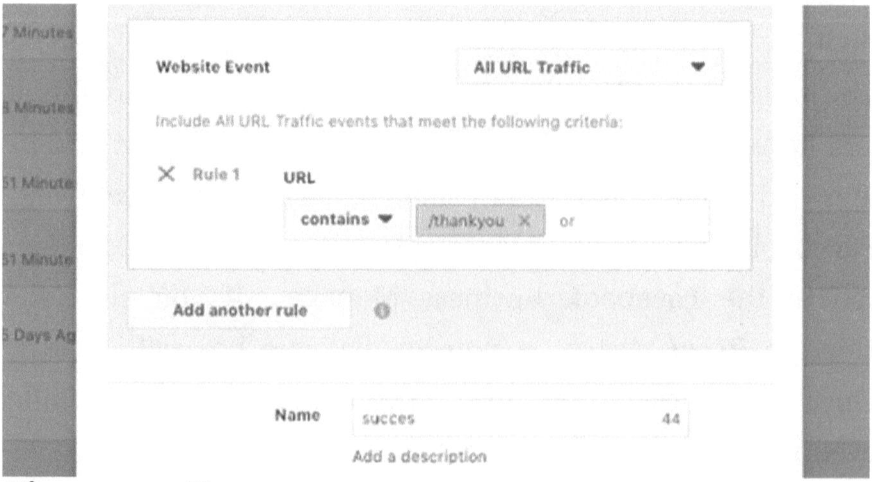

Figure 19: Events

Standard Events and Custom Conversions are both functions that can be used in Facebook Pixel. It has the same function in allowing you to track actions across your website. *Standard Events* gives you a more accurate data in terms of tracking and features. For example, if you use the Track Events on Inline Action, you'll get the exact number of customers that purchased your product. Additionally, you are given a choice to *Track Event on Page Load* or *Track Event on Inline Action*.

By clicking the first option, it will allow you to track the audiences who land on your page, or if you want to track those who completed a purchase in your audience. However, choose the second option if you want to track someone and require them to click something (e.g. Purchase button or Add to Cart).

Facebook also recommends adding event parameters like currency and conversion value if you want to measure additional information in your website. However, this setting is an optional setting, so you can skip this option if you want. On the other hand, *Custom Conversions* allows you to easily setup in Facebook Pixel, as it has no extra code needed. It can be created in Ads Manager by using the URL rules stated. However, unlike Standard Events, it may vary on the results of numbers. For example, if you had setup a conversion containing the word "New Year," it might also count results inside the website as: "Happy New Year" which may show different results. Lastly, after you have setup the Facebook Pixel on the Business Manager, you can copy the event code and paste it in your website code. Just make sure not to modify any pixel code given to you. If all of these notions look complicated for you, we recommend hiring a programmer to setup your Facebook Pixel.

While you are using the Facebook Pixel, **Landing Page Views** are counted to monitor how many people landed in your website after clicking the Ad. Landing Page Views are used to see how many people clicked for your Ads to directly go to the website. However, the setting is only possible if you have input a Facebook Pixel into your website.

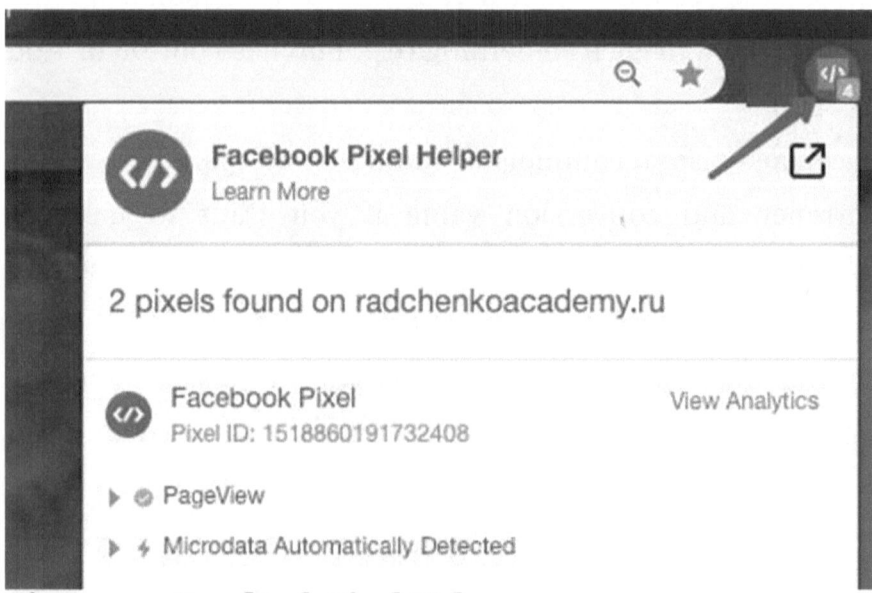

Figure 20: Facebook Pixel Helper

If Facebook Pixel is not working correctly, a tool called ***Facebook Pixel Helper*** can be downloaded as a troubleshooting tool to determine why your pixel is not working properly. It's a Chrome plug-in or an extension, as seen on the screenshot above, that can be used to see if there's a Facebook Pixel installed on your website. Thus, it creates reports on common errors such as: No Pixel Found, Pixel did not load, Not a standard event and etc. This tool serves its purpose by determining if your Pixel is functioning properly on your website. To install this extension, just search for the Facebook Pixel Helper in the Chrome web store. You must remember that this extension is only supported by Google Chrome, so make sure that you are using Chrome before you use the extension.

2.5 Conversions

For your campaign's effectiveness, you can use **Conversions** to drive more audience actions to your business. Conversion is an important type of objective that can directly give you a target audience, which will most likely purchase from your business. It is a type of objective that aims to make people do a specific action such as signing up for an e-mail subscription or purchase your product. This type of objective actually requires the use of Facebook Pixel or app events, which may help you to get more people to see your website.

In reality, conversion is more appropriate to businesses that have websites, especially if you want people to check out a product and view it in a particular page in your website. Platforms that support this kind of objective also encompass the same of traffic objective including: *Facebook, Instagram, Messenger* and *Audience Network*. Creating an advertisement in Facebook allows you to select the conversion objective itself by choosing if it can be available in your Website or Application. Moreover, you can also target people in the Audience section during your ad creation. Conversion objective has more advantage if your business requires an application to be installed because you can see the people who previously installed your application.

Just like other goals, Conversion uses **Facebook Algorithm** that works by looking for people who are most likely match on the interest of your business. This algorithm operates by collecting data through this objective and tries to analyze it to deliver the best results. The setup is called *Learning Phase*. As you choose the conversion objective, Facebook Algorithm will learn to show the Ads to various audience and tries to relate it as much as possible for your business. The algorithm helps you in advertising by showing your Ads to relevant people. More of the Learning Phase will be discussed later.

To create a custom conversion, go to the Ads Manager page and click the Create Custom Conversion button. Select the URL Contains portion and select Event. You may choose an event whether standard or custom. Then, choose your parameter. You can add several parameters by selecting End. You may be able to see different parameters depending on the Event that you have chosen. After setting the parameters, you may select a category for your custom conversion. Do not forget to click Next to create your conversion. You may also give your custom conversion a name and set a conversion value afterwards.

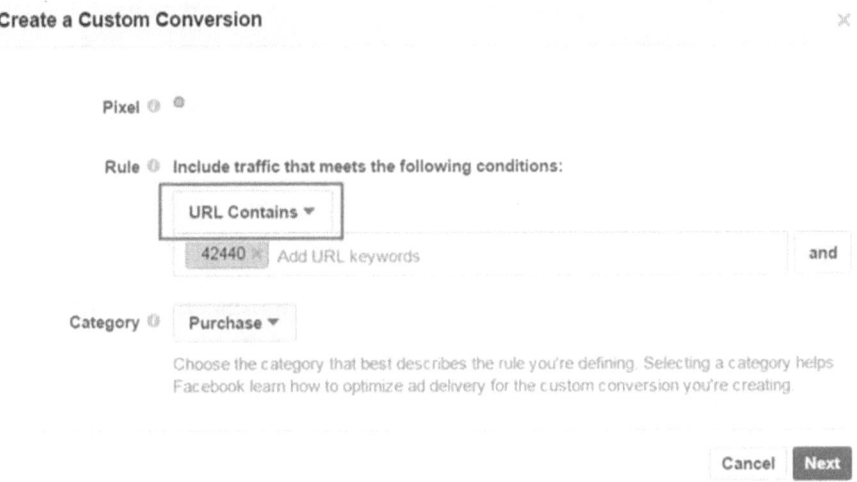

Figure 21: Custom Conversion

Make sure to check your website if the conversion is already activated. If it's not yet activated in the Custom Conversion page that you created and has a "No Activity Yet" Status, you may try to ensure that the URL has the Facebook Pixel installed on it. Try to use the Facebook Pixel Helper tool to check the problem for your conversion. Remember also that your URL on the conversion must be the same on the website.

Using a conversion objective is largely important in funneling strategy because it is mostly aligned with your goal which will lead people to register, purchase, download, or just visit your store.

2.6 Lead Generation

If you're not the type of business that has a website but you still want to drive people in your business, you may use the **Lead Generation** as one of your objectives in finding potential customers. Analyze first if your business is good for Lead Generation objective in order to know if you will be able to use it efficiently. Contemplate questions such as: Do you want people to register on your website? Do you Do you want users to sign up for updates from you? These inquiries may help you in knowing if you will be able to use Lead Generation.

You may employ this type of campaign if you want to create an Ad on Facebook and Instagram that collects information from people. The benefit of integrating the lead generation campaign allows you to have an instant data from your audience as they click your lead ad and prompted to fill out the necessary contact information. Lead Generation allows you to create *Lead Ads*. *Lead Ads* are ads that can be utilized to collect information through newsletter sign-ups, business information, contact form and others.

You can also customize the questions in the contact forms of your ad to align with your type of business. If you're wondering how you can get the reports from your Ads, you can collect it by exporting from your Page or through the Ads Manager under the Results column if you're using Facebook Business Manager. However, you must remember that ONLY page admins can download the leads. Other page roles won't be able to download the leads if they are not assigned as an administrator to the role. Only those users who are assigned to have permission in exporting the leads will have access to the report. Also note that you only have *90 days* to export your leads; otherwise, Facebook will automatically delete the reports due to both security and storage considerations, so you must regularly export your data as soon as possible. Unlike Conversions and Traffic Objective, lead generation is only supported by *Facebook, Instagram* and *Messenger*. Also, *Single Image, Single Video, Carousel* and *Slideshow* are the only ad formats in which you can choose in creating a lead generation objective.

To make it clearer, there is a huge difference between Lead Generation Ad and Conversion Ad. A Lead Ad doesn't need a Facebook Pixel to be used to gather information unlike Conversion Ads that needs to be setup on your website. Lead Ads generally collect data in Facebook through pop-up forms and generate its results on the Facebook Page. Meanwhile, Conversion Ads gather information through your own website and the forms are directly emailed to you.

Step 3: Choosing Your Audience

3.1 Targeting Options Overview

We formerly discussed in the previous lessons that you may choose your audience through the use of Ads Manager. During the creation of your Ad, we mentioned that you can edit the **Audience** section. Using this setting in the Ads Manager allows you to select various options in targeting the audience for your business. The options that you can use during the Ad Set creation include the following:

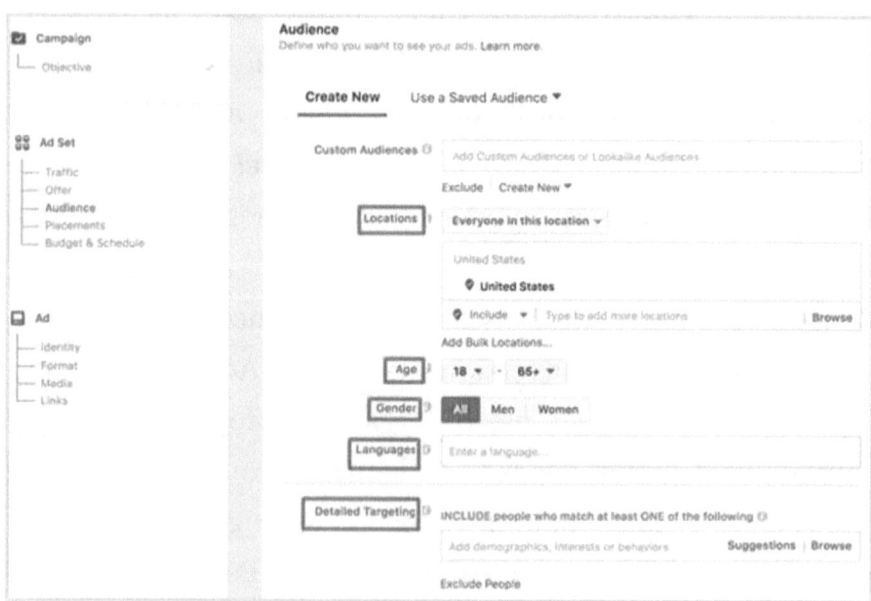

Figure 22: Audience Section

Locations – Location targeting is important for businesses especially for those that are involved in the e-commerce industry. You can target multiple countries for your advertisement using the Ads Manager. Options such as typing the words: Worldwide, Asia, iTunes, Toronto, and etc. can be used in the location targeting section. You can also Browse locations if you don't know which region or country to target. Moreover, you can also save the location list you have chosen for your future campaigns. Just make sure that you have created a list under the Saved Locations section in the Location section. However, the maximum number of Saved Locations you can have is 500, so verify, that your Ads comply with the laws and regulations of the targeted location especially since some regions have different advertising policies.

If you don't want to use the Ads Manager in location targeting, you can also go to your Facebook Page and click the Promote button on the left and edit the Audience Section to choose your target location.

Age – You can use this option to target people within an age range.

Gender – This setting allows you to target men, women or both for your business.

Languages – This option enables you to target certain users in other languages.

Detailed Targeting – A setting that assists you with choosing an additional demographic information, interests and behaviors for your target audience. It is an enhanced version of targeting as it is a more precise way of pursuing an audience.

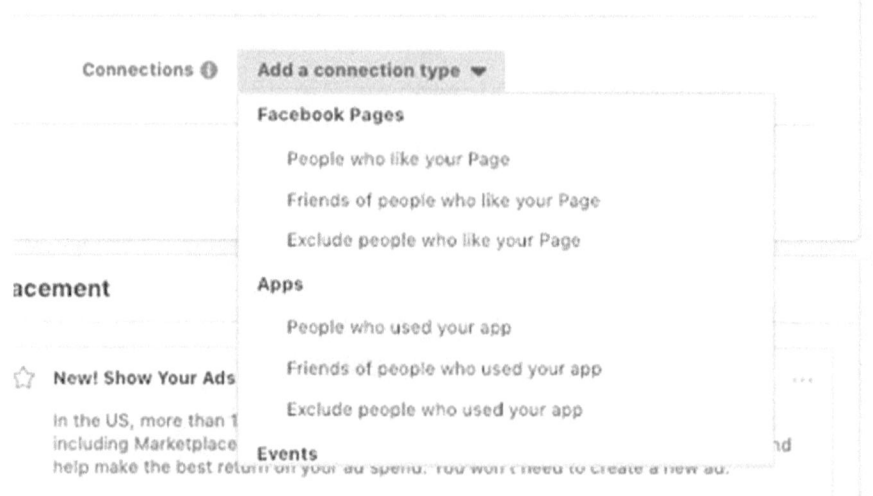

Figure 23: Connection Targeting

Connections – This type of targeting helps you to find potential customers related to your business. It is located at the "Connections" sub-section during the Ad Set creation. Connection targeting will pinpoint your advertisement to people who are connected to the Page, App or Event in the Facebook Platform. Once a person is engaged in one of the means given, even their friends can see the advertisement. Clicking the Advanced Combination button allows you to include or exclude several connections, depending on your campaign objective. This capability will allow you to set up series of criteria for a person to be able to be considered as your audience for your advertisement. However, you must remember not to set too many parameters as also cited in the Detailed Targeting. Multiple Parameters are not recommended because the combinations for the connections maybe too narrow to be effective for the audience. Widening the connection is one of the best options to make it more effective for the audience.

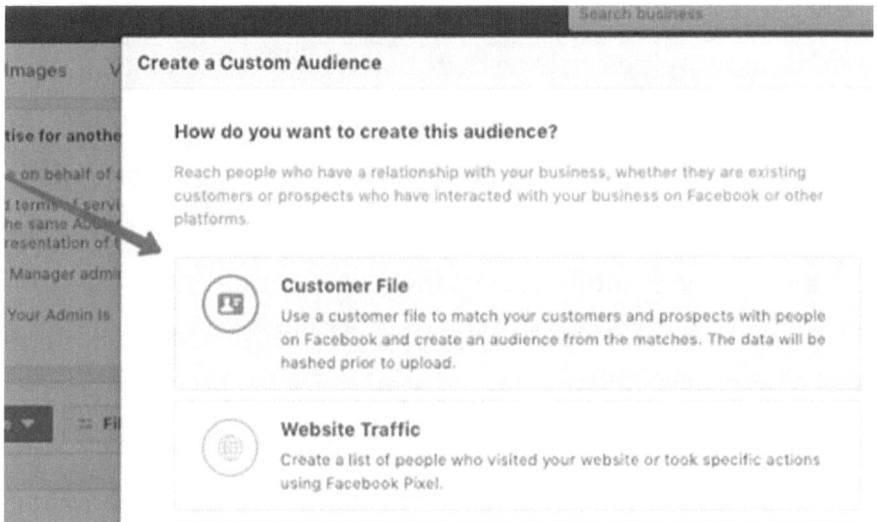

Figure 24: Custom Audience

Custom Audiences – These are audiences based from the information you have given to Facebook during the Ad creation. You can custom the audiences using various platforms such as Facebook Pixel.

3.1.1 Detailed Targeting

Options that are available for detailed targeting might be based on several factors. Ads that people click, Pages that they usually engage with, Demographics like age, gender and location, Mobile device that they use & the speed of their network connection, and Activities people engage in on and off Facebook like their travel preferences, and purchase behaviors may be an option for detailed targeting. However, if these options are not suitable for your business, you can browse the full list of the detailed targeting options using the "Add demographics, interests or behaviors" search bar.

The interests for the perspective of the potential targets in detailed targeting plays an important role. In fact, if you don't understand who will potentially see your advertisement, then you are in big trouble. Analyzing the common denominator for your visitors might help you to know which certain interests they want for your business. To achieve this goal, you may go to the Pages of famous brands that are in line with your business. Doing this will make you avoid choosing general interest options in detailed targeting. You must also think outside the box. Brainstorm other related markets that you can use to target other customers. For example, if you're in the camping business, you may also target those people who like outdoor activities.

3.1.2 Custom Audiences

There are several types of Custom Audience that you can create.

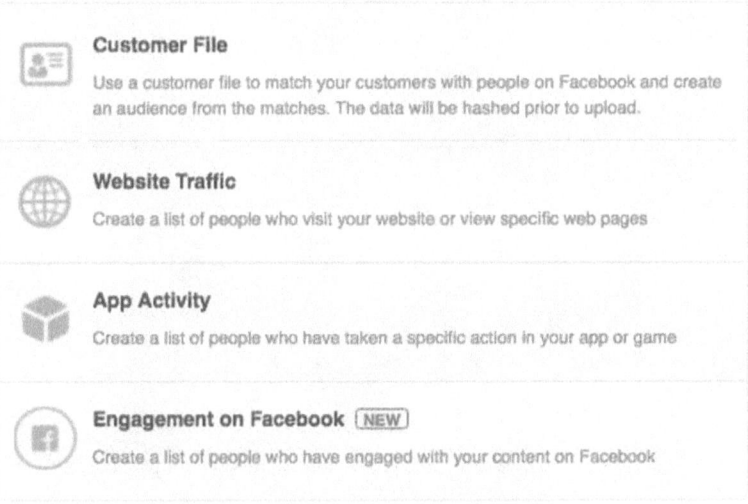

Figure 25: Type of Custom Audience

Custom Audiences from a customer list is the first type of Custom Audience. Choosing this option will allow you to import your own file in the Custom Audience Section.

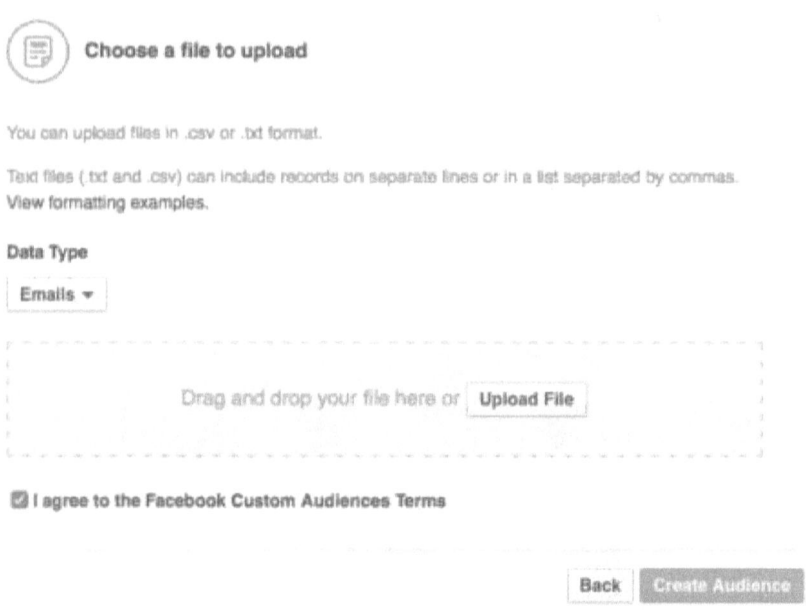

Figure 26: Customer List Uploading

As you can see, it will allow you to upload a customer file. These can be names or e-mail addresses of the customers that are engaged in your business. After uploading the file, edit data mapping would be the next option. Three statuses would be seen during the preview. The green check mark indicates that Facebook understands the data while the orange exclamation point means that Facebook is not sure of the type of data. However, the red exclamation icon means that the data has been identified as unsupported format. To address this problem, you must select from the dropdown option and choose **Do Not Upload.** This will tell Facebook not to use the data when matching for audiences. The data can also be formatted through choosing the **Choose Format** dropdown. This will make Facebook understand what format they need to use to match for your data. Using this type of custom will also enable Facebook to upload the data as they understand it and create an audience for you.

Engagement Custom Audiences is the second type of Custom Audience. This type of custom is used for people who have engaged with the contents of your business in Facebook, including pages, apps and your services or products. The custom also refers to audiences who spend their time viewing your posts and watching your videos.

You must remember that there is a difference between this custom and ***Custom Audiences from your website.***

Both of the type of customs audiences use engagement for your advertisements. However, Custom Audiences from your website is used to target audiences in your website and can be tracked using Pixel. Engagement Custom Audiences on the other hand, targets audiences that engaged in your Facebook pages or services.

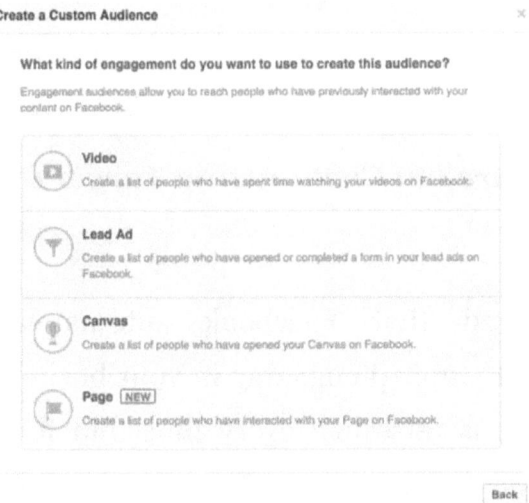

Figure 27: Custom Audience

By choosing this custom, you may also tell Facebook how many days you want them to collect the engagement. For example, if you select 10 days ago, Facebook will target audiences who engaged in your business 10 days ago up to the present.

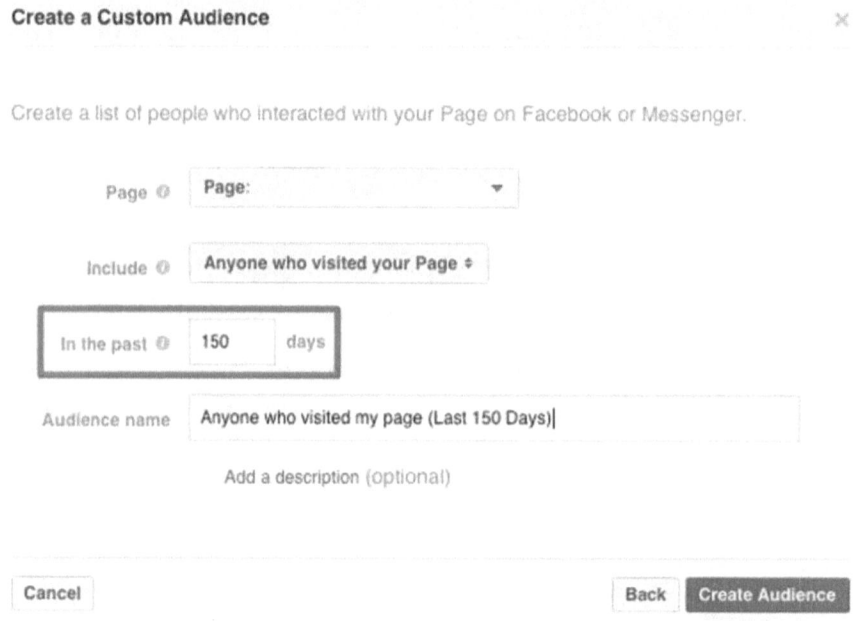

Figure 28: Customizing Target Days

Keep in mind that Facebook automatically removes audiences that stopped engaging in your business. In reality, your audience is refreshed every time, but it doesn't mean that you need to create or edit new Engagement Custom Audiences.

Website Custom Audience. As suggested earlier, this type of custom audience uses engagement from your website.

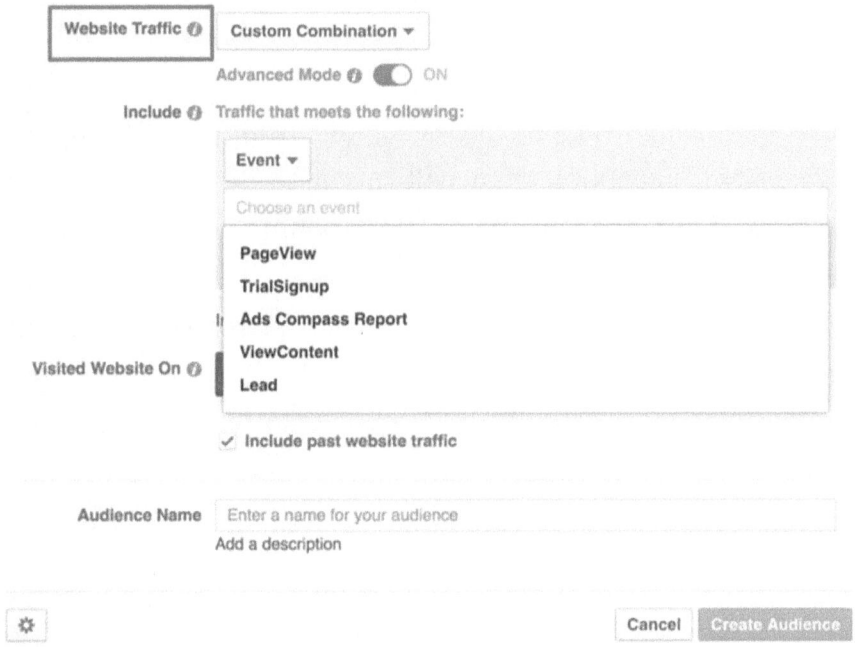

Figure 29: Website Custom Audience

Using this option will allow you to create a Custom Audience for people who visit your website and you would like to reach. Like engagement in Facebook, you may also customize this type by selecting how many days you want Facebook to collect the engagement. The benefit of adding this type of custom audience in Pixel will enable you to reach those people who visited or viewed your product on your website but didn't push through with the purchase.

Mobile App Custom Audiences is the last type of custom audience that you can choose. This setting is used to create a custom audience for your App Ad. Facebook SDK or Facebook Software Development Kit is usually used by developers in creating applications. This tool is largely used to pass the data to Facebook. If you want to use the data to tell Facebook who you want to include in your custom audience through those Traffics in your App Ad, you may use this custom. Facebook then will target those audiences who will likely download the app or those people who downloaded it but had merely minimal engagement. To create custom audience for your App Ad, you must first register your app and set up the SDK to log the app events. It is recommended to seek the help of a developer for this step. Thus, it will allow you to create your Custom Audience. After setting up your Custom Audience in the Ads Manager, you may start running the mobile app engagement ads.

3.1.3 Lookalike Audiences

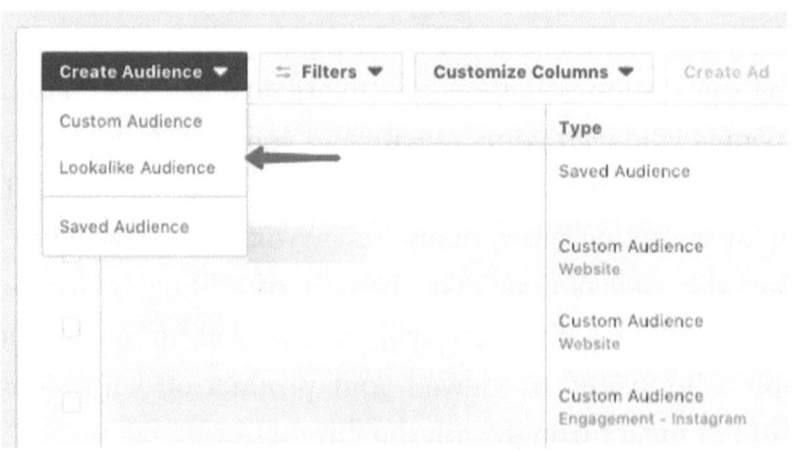

Figure 30: Lookalike Audience

Lookalike Audience are the type of audiences that Facebook reaches through your advertisement with the same interest as those people who are engaged in your business. Most likely, these are the people who are similar to your current customers. They can be people from the country/countries you have selected or from smaller audience reach if you want to narrow down your ad reach. This feature is very useful if you want to be somehow precise in targeting your audience. Your Ads will be seen by fewer people depending on the number of your lookalikes, but they yield a higher chance of making the audience reach and interact with your business.

You may create up to 500 Lookalike Audiences during the creation of your Ad and may be able to create multiple Lookalike Audiences at the same time in a single Ad. To devise a Facebook Lookalike Audience, you may go to your Audiences in the Business Manager and click the "Create Audience" dropdown option. Choose the "Lookalike Audience" option then select your source. You must remember that a source may be from your created Custom Audience. Then, you may select the country/countries where you want your Ad to be seen. After setting up your lookalike audiences, wait until 24 hours for your audience to be created in Facebook. Keep in mind that creating a larger audience means a larger reach for your advertisement, but it will lessen the chance of creating a lookalike audience. Meanwhile, if you create a smaller scale, it will increase the accuracy of getting a similar audience thus, creating a better effectivity for your advertisements. It is recommended to source an audience between 1,000 – 50,000 for better results. In addition, the best lookalike audiences that you can put are those people who purchase products related to your business, your regular customers' characteristics, or those with higher incomes.

You may upload the email addresses of your existing customers or telephone numbers for estimating your lookalike audiences through the Create New drop-down arrow. Use also the slider as a percentage range of the population that you want to target of the chosen country or location if you can't source the audience from email addresses or telephone numbers.

3.2 How to Target Audience with High Income?

Not everyone can afford a certain product, especially if it's premium or has an above average price tag. Thus, targeting an audience with higher income is essential to avoid spending too much in advertising on the wrong reach of audience. As discussed, a while ago, you may customize audiences depending on your needs. Using detailed targeting and other type of custom audiences is important in targeting audience with high income. Think of premium products that either related or not in your product. Use these products as a basis for your own target. For example, if you're business is about gadgets, you may take Iphone as a basis for your audience. Objectively, those people who uses this brand are most likely people who have higher income given the price of a single Iphone. In other words, those people who are already working. During the Audience creation in the Ads Manager, you may input specific locations of places that are considered as business districts like New York City. Doing so will increase your chance to reach people who are working. Moreover, ages and gender do matter too. Based on our example, you may input 25-50 years old for the age and All for the gender since Iphone may be used by those types of people. You may also use detailed targeting for this. Going back to our example about Iphone, you can input the words "Owns: Iphone" in the section to accurately reach those people.

3.3 Cold, Warm and Hot Audiences

Like the seasons, marketing has its own seasons too and knowing it will increase your chance in targeting your audience efficiently. There is a term called ***Traffic Temperature,*** which online businesses use to categorize audiences and relate them with their business. There are three stages in traffic:

- *Cold Audience* – This type of audiences are those that are aware of your business but not ready to purchase your product. They might have a little knowledge of your product but are not ready to engage with it. Your aim is to increase your temperature scale to Warm by reaching to specific audience who are most likely to deal with your product.

- *Warm Audience* – This audience are people who somehow knows your business and maybe interacted with your business but not occasionally. They are not considered as customers since they haven't bought anything yet from your business. You can consider them as people who are interested in your business and potential buyers. To convert these people to Hot Audiences, you must spend more money by convincing them to buy your product. Analyze why they are just interested in your business but haven't committed to purchasing. As long as you are doing your best, this kind of traffic is something that you can control since you have a semi-relationship with them.
- *Hot Audience* – This audience are people who knows your business, recognized what your products or services are for. These types are also ones that you already have interacted with. Meaning to say, you own this traffic and you already have built trust and relationships with your audience. These audiences have higher chance of buying your products again in the future. You also have direct access to them through their contacts. It is also easy to reach them since you've already established your business.

It is the best to always set your goal in getting into Hot Temperature since they reflect those audiences who will increase your sales. Don't forget to also target your Warm Audiences. The potential is there and it is up to you concerning how you will act to make them your customers.

3.4 Excluding and Narrowing the Audience

One good aspect about detailed targeting is that you can also include or exclude people for your advertisement. Literally, detailed targeting offers 2 main actions which is the *Include People option* and *Exclude People*. *Excluding People* would most likely remove those audiences under the characteristics that your will provide. *Include People* will add audiences with those characteristics whether or not it is related to your business. The benefit of using this feature in the Audience section makes you more specific in targeting your audience. It will increase the chance of targeting audiences who are most likely will buy your products in the future.

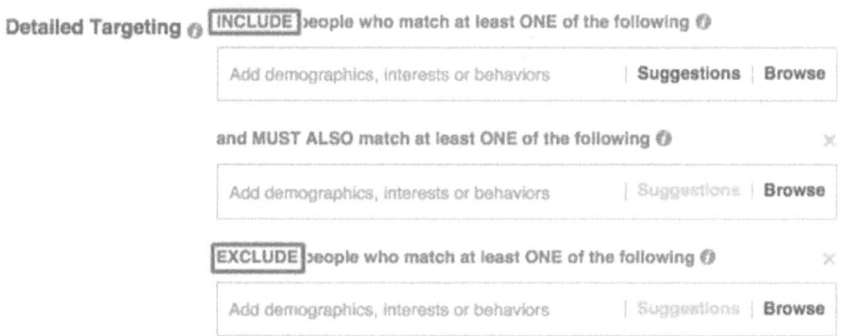

Figure 31: Including & Excluding People

To use this efficiently in the Audience Section, you may choose the Detailed Targeting option in the Ad creation. Choose whether you want to *Include people* or *Exclude People*. By adding criteria to these fields, you must include the words "or" and "and". Thus, you must analyze first if what will be more relevant for your business. For example, if you're in the clothing business and included "Forever 21 and Uniqlo," your Ad will target those people who had liked both Forever 21 and Uniqlo. Using "And" is much more recommended as it will target more audience.

Narrowing audiences, on the other hand, is an additional option that you can use to further specify in targeting your audience. By clicking Narrow Audience option, you may narrow the audiences based on your desire characteristics. Select "Narrow it further" if you want to be more specific and detailed. For example, you have used the Excluding option to exclude audiences who loves painting, you may further narrow it down by adding an "and" or "or" word into the phrase. Going back to an example, it will look like this: "Exclude Audiences who love painting and are under 18 years old and female."

Giving yourself flexibility is main suggestion in Excluding and Narrowing your audiences. Being so specific might result in negative results for your advertisements in the future.

You may also combine certain options in detailed targeting such as excluding and narrowing at the same time. The words "and" and "or" may also be combined in detailed targeting.

For example: Exclude people who eat pork or eat beef and working people. In this sentence, you can see that it uses "or" for people who love pork and beef. Those people who eat pork and work would be excluded in your advertisements.

Being specific helps you to target down perfect audience for your ads. However, be careful not to be too much specific when narrowing your audience as it will affect the number of reach for your advertisement. We recommend making your audience broad but specific to reach the right amount of people.

3.5 Placements and Devices

Placement is a term used to let Facebook show your Ads in the best places where they think your business will benefit much. It also refers to the places where you make your Ads run. Using placements helps you to reach people through certain places in Facebook where you think they usually spend their time. Availability of placements depends on your chosen objective. The placements that may be available for you encompass these:

- ***Facebook*** – Your Ads may appear in the News Feed of people accessing this website on laptops or desktop computers. Those who are using their mobile devices to browse their News Feed will also be your audience. Ads may also appear in several places on Facebook, such as to the right column of those users who are accessing Facebook on their computers, to Marketplace homepage and lastly, as *In-stream video,* which allows users to see your Ads as short videos.

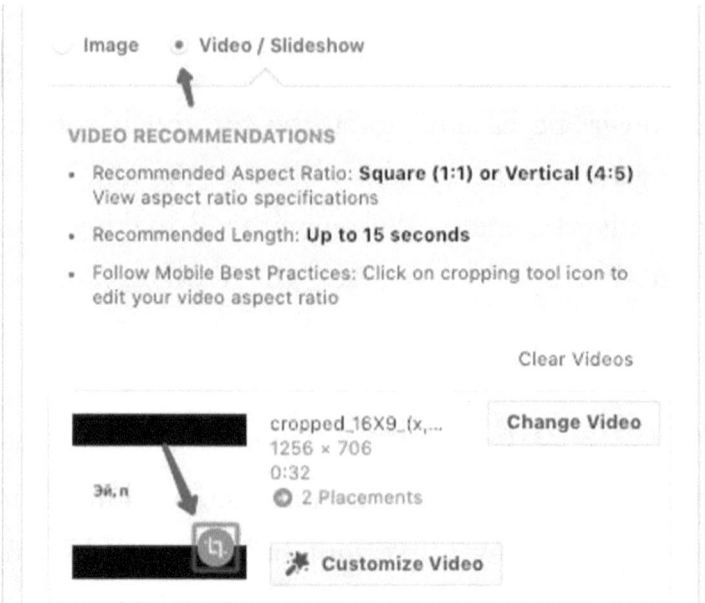

Figure 32: Video Ads

In-stream video enables you to show 5-15 seconds mini-roll video Ads to audiences that watched videos on Facebook and through Audience Network. This Ad placement may be available in Ads Manager. Use Video views, brand awareness, app install, reach and engagement as objectives to allow In-stream video placements for your advertisements. To continue creating this kind of placement, choose **Automatic Placements** or **Edit Placements** in the *Placement Section*. Choosing Automatic Placements will automatically include In-stream video on other placements for the delivery of your Ad. On the other hand, choosing Edit Placement can allow you to select In-stream video, along with other placements.

You must also remember that depending on the audience's interests, users might see different Ads on Facebook.

Figure 33: Instagram Ads

- **Instagram** – Your Ads may appear in the desktop feed of those people accessing Instagram through their laptops or desktops. For people using the Instagram app in their mobile devices or mobile browser, your Ads will also be placed. Like Messenger, Facebook may also situate your Ads on Instagram Stories.

- *Messenger* – Since this app acts separately on Facebook, Facebook also places Ads on Messenger. Ads may be placed in the Home Tab of Messenger or your Inbox section. If a person has an existing conversation with your business, your Ads may be directly delivered to him or her. Lastly, your Ads may be placed on people's stories tab in Messenger.

- *Audience Network* – This type of placement works beyond the Facebook platform. The benefit of using Audience Network lets advertisers increase the number of places for their advertisements in the internet. Audience Network uses the same targeting, auction, delivery and measurement systems like Facebook ads. Additionally, this kind of placement allows user to show their ads through other websites and applications that are supported by Facebook.

  Native Ads – a type of audience network ad format that looks like a part of your app or site when displayed to the audience.

  Interstitial Ads – these are full-screen ads that appear on sites or apps during transitions between tasks.

Banner Ads – this type of ad appears at the top or bottom of the screen. They are usually smaller than full-screen ads. Facebook tends to perceive this kind of ad format as the least performing of all because people usually ignore it.

In-stream Video Ads – these ads may be in pre-roll, mid-roll and post-roll in a video player on a website. Meaning to say, this ad format can run before, during a break, or after a video content. As previously stated, it will require you to integrate the Audience Network with your video player.

Rewarded Video Ads – this type of ad format can be used for gaming apps. It works with those audiences who play a game and get a reward in exchange for watching a video ad.

It is recommended to choose the placement of your ad to your desired format that you think will work efficiently in promoting your business. For example, if you're into the food business, consider choosing Instagram format ads as they promote pictures effectively to viewers. Doing so will increase your chance to reach potential customers. You may choose to edit the placement as seen on the picture:

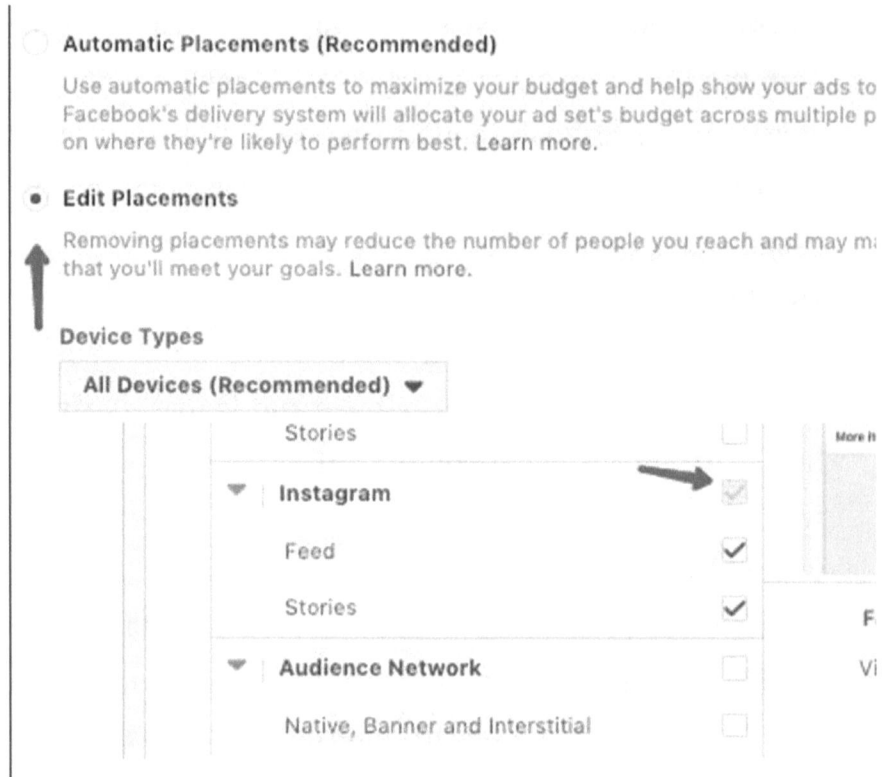

Figure 34: Edit Placements

Devices that users use are important to consider when creating an Ad. In fact, people vary in using devices when browsing the social media. Some people use their laptops, desktop computers and mobile phone when browsing Facebook. However, according to the latest Facebook Statistics in 2018, 88% of Facebook users use their mobile phones in browsing. This means that targeting people who use their mobile phones is relevant for your business.

In terms of using your ads to devices efficiently, choosing ad formats that support mobile devices will be effective for your business. Several tips will be given to help you in choosing audiences for your ad.

Make every means to make your ad benefit the user. When creating your Ad, make it in a way that the captions will compel the audience to click right away. Remember that mobile devices have limited screen unlike computers. So be specific and clear when making an Ad.

Make your Ad short as possible. No one wants to read a long caption in mobile devices as it will occupy the whole screen. Facebook automatically shortens long captions and will add "continue reading" link on your Ads. You may still place long captions if you want to share a story but ensure that the first paragraph will catch the audience's attention and make them read all the captions.

Mobile Optimized Landing Page is a recommended action. When you suggest a link or post on your Ads, people may click the link anytime. Thus, if they are using mobile phones and your link is not optimized on mobile devices, the link may not work properly on their devices. You may optimize landing page by using external software packages such as Instapage and Lander App.

3.6 Budgeting and Scheduling

Your budget in ad campaigning is really critical as it will help you to know how you will maximize your advertisements in Facebook. Setting a budget before you proceed with the campaign is actually a smart move, so that you will not lose control on the costs of every advertisement you are making on Facebook. In this way, you can avoid overspending and also save some money for your business. You must remember that setting a budget doesn't mean that you are not buying an Ad or you don't have the capacity to show your Ads but rather, you are telling Facebook that this estimate is merely your budget for the Ads placement.

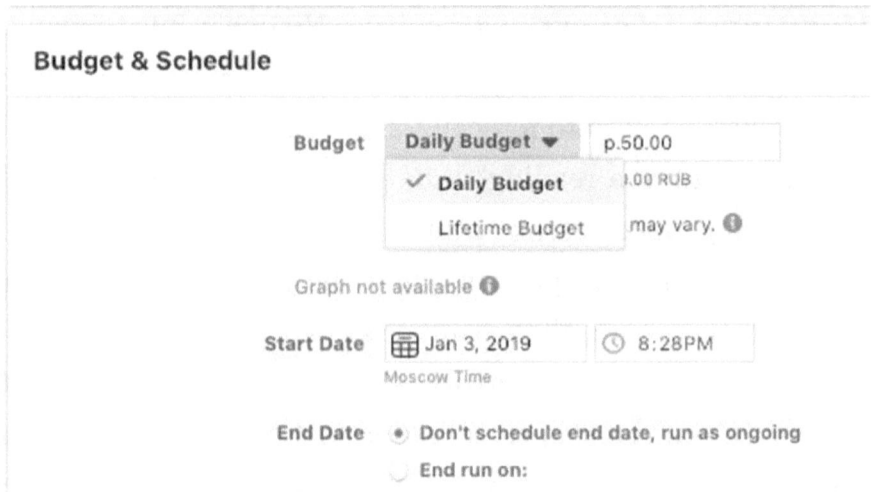

Figure 35: Choosing Budget

Facebook actually offers two types of budgets that you can set during the Ad Set or in the Campaign level mentioned earlier. The first one is the **Daily Budget.** By selecting the Daily Budget setting, it will tell Facebook the average amount you are willing to spend on a daily basis for your advertisement. However, if you're not into setting it on a daily basis, you can choose **Lifetime Budgets** to establish the amount you are willing to spend during your entire ad campaign. However, kindly note that you can't switch the budget type after you've already created your ad set or campaign, but you can still duplicate your existing ad set or campaign, so you can change the budget type and the amount if you want. This option will allow you to create a new ad set or campaign.

For additional information, amounts for the budget can also be changed anytime. Just go to the Ads Manager on your Facebook Business Manager then hover to the Ad Set or Campaign you made and click edit. After changing the amount, you can confirm it. Wait fifteen minutes so Facebook can apply and update the budget that you have set. However, for some time, your ads will pause as soon as you have changed the amount. Make sure to wait fifteen minutes to unpause it in the Ad set or Campaign tabs so it will not confuse the Facebook System. Changing the budget will also prompt the Facebook System to re-learn delivering your Ads to the platform. Thus, it will also impact the performance on your Ad Placements. Raising the budget doesn't mean that the performance will get better as there are factors such as poor targeting and Ad creativity that are affecting your campaign. However, increasing the budget could lead to more results as it can widen the reach of its audience. Meanwhile, lowering the budget can lead to fewer results due to the decrease of the audience reach. If you're thinking of recommending an exact budget that you can use for your advertisement, it actually depends on your decision about how much you want to spend for your campaign. What is important is that you have a budget in mind that will help you during your entire campaign.

On the other hand, you may schedule your Ads in the Ad Set creation. **Scheduling** allows you to control both the dates and times you want to show your Ads. To schedule ads, you may go to the Ads Manager and click Ad Sets. You will see under the Budget & Schedule section the *Schedule Start* and *Schedule End*. These settings allow you to set the date and schedule for your Ads. If you have a lifetime budget, schedule your Ad Set to run on a specific date and time. Remember that your Ad must at least run for an hour. After your schedule has been completed, you may extend the date of your completed ad through the ads manager by editing the Ad Set.

Step 4: Creating an Effective Ad

4.1 What Ad Formats are the Most Effective?

Earlier, you were introduced briefly about the different ad placements on Facebook. This lesson will discuss the Ad formats thoroughly. The Facebook platform has 3 primary Facebook ad placements.

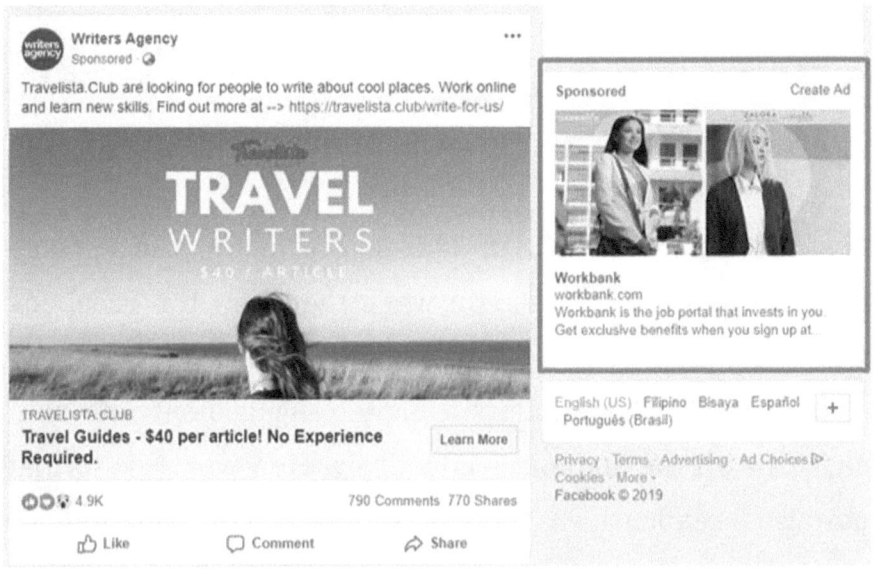

Figure 36: Right Column Ad Sample

The first placement is the **Right Column Ad**. This format appears on the right side of the News Feed of a user. It's the most traditional format but still used until today. If you want to make this effective for your ad, make it as relevant as possible to the users. Good visual and call-to-action ads will also increase your chance to receive a visit from an audience.

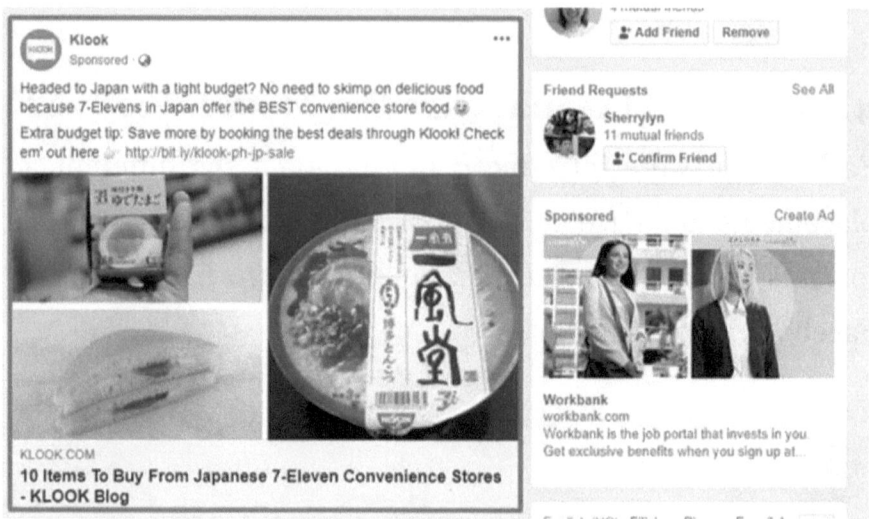

Figure 37: Desktop Newsfeed Ad Sample

Desktop News Feed Ad. This second placement appears in the News Feed of a person when they view the Facebook page on laptop or desktop computer. Based on others' experiences, this type offers a higher engagement rate as it engages with the audiences effectively. However, this format may also be expensive.

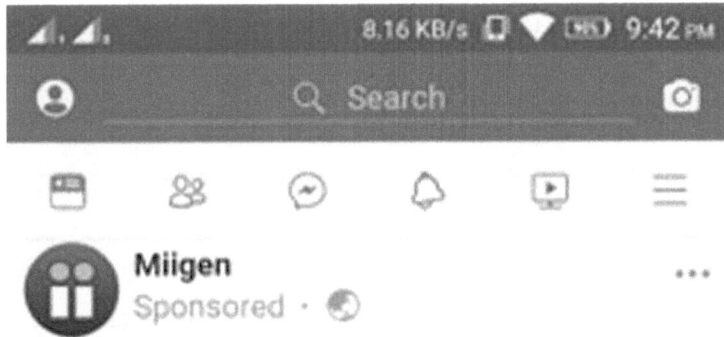

Figure 38: Mobile Newsfeed Ad Sample

Lastly, as listed previously, **Mobile News Feed Ad** is also available to attract an audience. Using formats such as Video Ad, Call-to-action and other formats may be used in Mobile News Feed Ad.

In terms of rating the placements, we must say that every placement is effective as it functions differently with others. The most important focus in creating an effective ad is the content of the ad itself. This is the reason why Ad formats come in a variety. There are several formats that can contribute in the effectivity of your ads. These are: Photo ads, multi product ads, call-to-action ads and event ads.

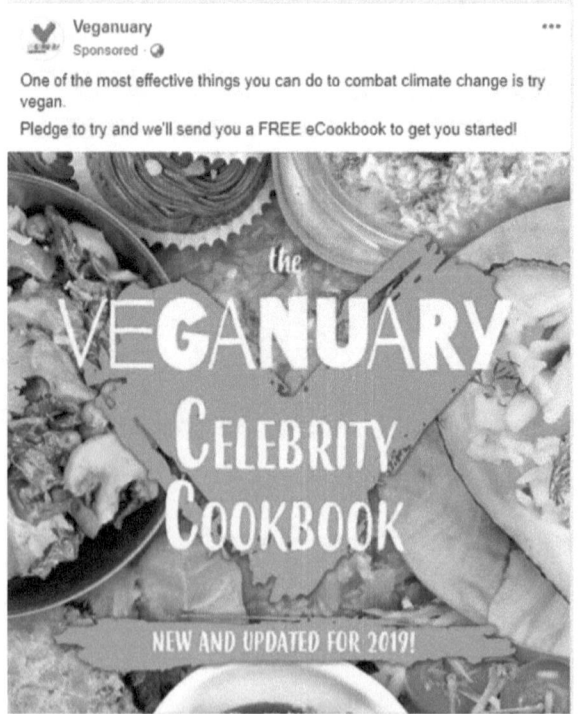

Figure 39: Photo Ad Sample

Photo Ad is a very effective type of advertisement because people are very visual. You may use it through that 3 primary Ad placements that are stated earlier. Make sure to utilize an image that tells exactly what your product is. It is better to be honest than to risk losing the trust of your audience. Putting pictures with your advertisement can increase brand awareness to your audience. Especially if you're in the food business, putting an eye-catching, delicious picture of your product can attract potential customers to your business. Keep in mind that we always say in this book that your end goal is to make them buy your product!

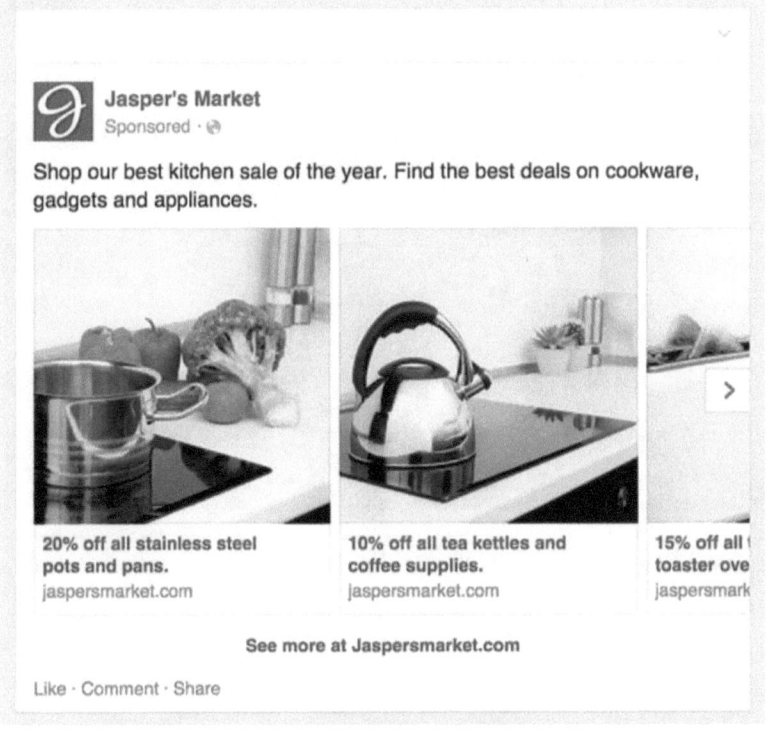

Figure 40: Photo Ad Sample

Multi Product Ad format allows you to show multiple products at the same time in one ad. The audience can scroll horizontally the images and click on it individually. These are effective usually to businesses who are in line with food or online shops. This format is also recommended to businesses that have several products in their companies. The success of this format depends on the multiple pictures that you will input in the Ad. Make sure that every picture is engaging and will not make the viewer lose one's interest while scrolling on your ad.

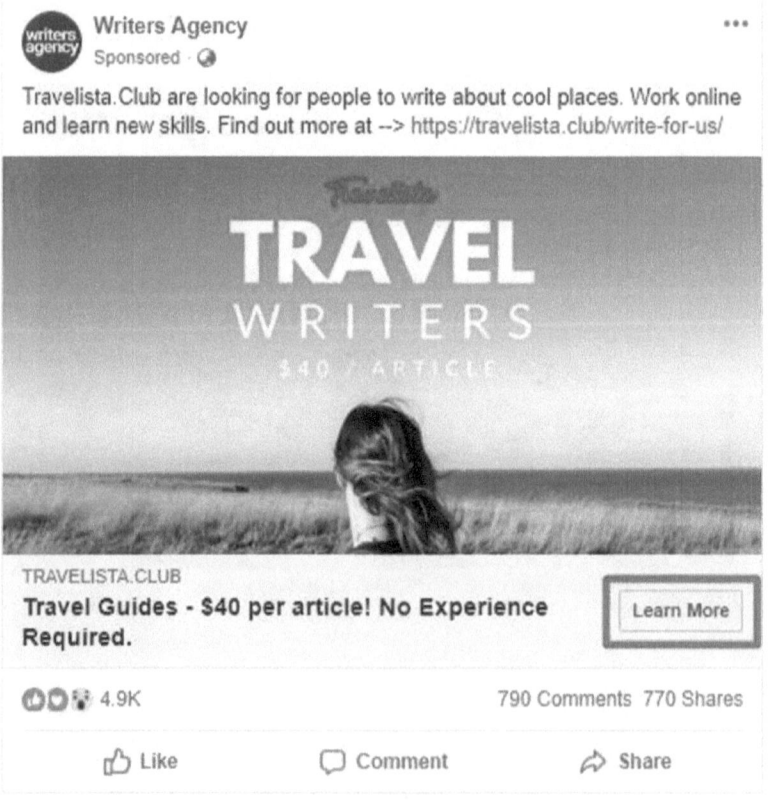

Figure 41: Call-to-action Ad Sample

Call-to-action Ad, on the other hand, signifies those that allow users to directly take an action to your ads. These are effective for businesses that offers something for their services or products. For example, if you're offering a discount for a certain time. Use this type of format, as stated in the traffic objective earlier. They are also effective for businesses that want to promote directions to their shops. This type of format is strongly advocated in every type of business, especially if you want the viewers to learn more about your products or services.

Figure 42: Event Ad Sample

Events Ad is another type of format that you can use to promote a specific event for your business. For example, you are promoting a discount event or giveaway event for your business, you may use this type of Ad format to promote your event.

Effectiveness of an advertisement depends on how visual and relevant your advertisements are. Make sure that your advertisements always look valuable from the audience's perspective.

Ranking the formats, it is recommended to use *Call-to-action Ad* along with *Photo Ad* to attract customers. These can be placed on desktop news feed, right column and mobile devices. Thus, the effectivity of using this ad format is high since you can place it everywhere. The next most effective format is the *Multi-product Ad*. It is beneficial since it allows users to see several products at the same time which increases their curiosity or interests in your business. Additionally, if you combine your multi-product ad with a call to action, it will be a perfect combination in the eyes of your viewers. Lastly, the least recommended format is the Event Ad since this is usually used for a particular season. If you want to make your ad appropriate for any time of the year especially if you are not promoting any event for your business, Event Ad is not recommended.

4.2 How to Design a Good Ad Banner Easily?

Ad banners are type of advertisement that delivers an Ad through websites. Its sole purpose is to attract traffic on your website when a person clicks the banner itself. Ad banners may come in variety of looks but still share the same function. When a person clicks on the image of the ad banner, he or she will be redirected to the website of the advertiser or the landing page.

Ad banners may come in different sizes of length and width. *Standard Banner* is 320x50. This is recommended to use for mobile phones. *Large Banner* on the other hand, is best used for tablets and larger devices as it has a size of 320x90. The last size of Facebook Ad Banner is the *Medium Rectangle*. They are recommended for scrollable feeds and end-of-level screens. The size of this banner is 300x250.

If you want to create an Ad Banner, you may use free or paid tools that can be searched through Google. There are benefits of using these websites. Using pre-made templates can help you to create an eye-catching ads easier. Websites such as: Bannersnack, Crello and Canva are only few of the websites that can be used to create banner ads. Also, keep in mind that banners have sizes as stated earlier. Thus, putting too many texts on it, aside from images, may stifle the effectiveness of your advertisement. We advise to put minimal words as much as possible but appealing at the same time. Keep in mind that the text must not be more than 20% of the banner screen. Using taglines would also help to increase the catch of your banners. You may check your creation through the Facebook Text Overlay Tool to see if you are having too much text on your Ad.

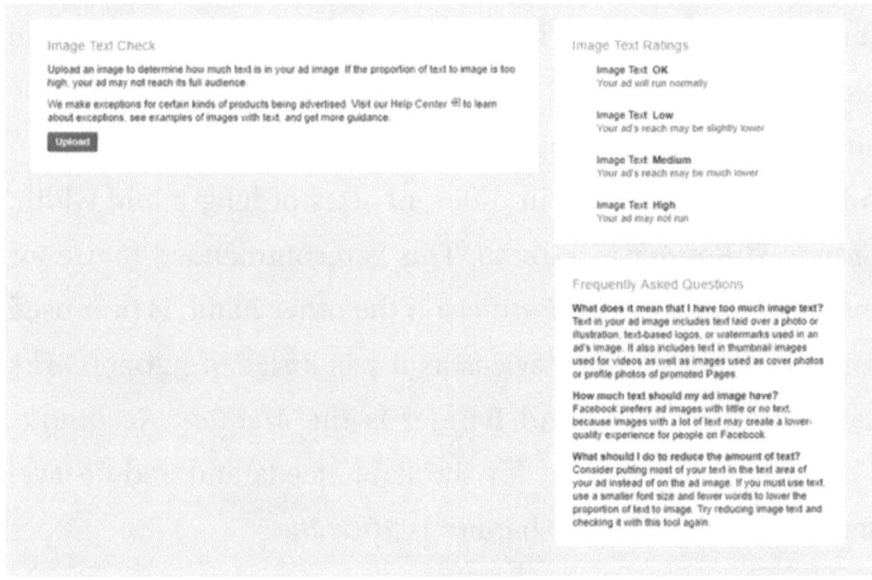

Figure 43: Facebook Overlay Tool

The good feature about Facebook is that it supports banner ads for your business through the Audience Network. However, adding banner ads may be a bit complicated as they require one to code input through the Facebook SDK (Software Developer Kit). Since Facebook allows advertisers to create banner ads in their apps, it is recommended to seek the help of a developer in implementing this kind of advertisement.

4.3 How to Write a Good Text

One of the reasons why advertisers fail in promoting their business is because of unattractive texts. Good pictures do speak, but texts make it clearer. This reason justifies why adding an effective text is important. However, there are times when the caption doesn't attract or the texts in the ads itself is boring. Thus, to avoid these situations, here are some tips that may help you in writing a good text for your ad.

Be personal with your audience. We have stated earlier about ways of narrowing your audience. Thus, you can use this technique to be more personal to them. For example, if you have narrowed your audience to those who are interested in health care, you may write related topics about it. It's more likely to speak then to those certain audiences. Just be careful not make it too personal in a way that will narrow your reach too much.

Try to write different captions for different people. If you are in a business that has several product lines, a single text may be hard to do. For example, if you are in a clothing business, you may try to write differently for men's and women's clothes. Doing so may make your ad more personal.

Do not over use the call-to-action. Since Facebook adds the button for action on your advertisement, you do not need to emphasize it so much in your captions. If the call-to-action already stated "Learn More," do not put the same words in your caption. You may use different texts indeed such as

"Find out why" instead of putting the same words in your Ad. Thus, it will still lead the audience to select your advertisement.

Keep it short. We've already mentioned in the previous chapter that keeping the text short is important. Make sure that even if it's one sentence caption, the words are engaging and pleasing to the eye!

Make it easy to understand. Do not use highfalutin words when writing. Make sure that the words are not deep and conversational. Doing so will make the viewers feel like you are talking to them. People will tend to ignore your Ad if you put words that they don't understand. Try to also show it to a few people to obtain feedback if your Ads are easy to understand.

4.4. What should You Know about Video Ads

Video advertisement is one of the most effective ways of campaigning for your business. In fact, 2017 Forbes Statistics have shown that 64% of people who watched a video ad tend to purchase the product displayed to them. Given the billions of people who watch Youtube every single day, this exposure means that video promotions are really an effective strategy. Hubspot Statistics in 2018 also revealed that selling platforms such as eBay and Amazon uses video ad for their products to increase the chance of the audience in buying by 35%.

The technology today is also advancing. Thus, businesses have seized the opportunity to market their business in every aspect. Using technology as their advantage, they let other people share and promote their products through videos. This happens when a person clicked the "share button" on your Facebook posts and even in other social media sites. Believe it or not, people who most likely to share contents with videos in them. Again, people are really visual after all and like to see things clearer through watching.

Aside from the power of Video Ads for people, one benefit of using Video Ads may include informing people through a creative way. Video Ads may help to educate people without them noticing that you are incorporating your products to them. Using How-to videos to help the viewers to address a concern may also increase your relationship. Aside from educating them, you can also build trust with your potential customers.

The difference in using Video Ads and Picture Ads is huge. In terms of promotion, video Ads allows you to thoroughly promote your product in a single video and in a short time. Picture Ads on the other hand, enable you to give a short glimpse of your business. Since picture ads usually have limited space, you can only put short texts on them and might not explain the nature of your business clearly.

To create a Video Ads for Facebook, you may follow these tips. First, **Decide on your customer avatar.** Customer avatar is also similar to a buyer persona. However, you are just relating it to the video that you wanted to produce. For example, if you want to create a video about Fitness & Health, your customer avatar could be athletes, a housewife who is interested in fitness, and health conscious people. Also, include the demographics, along with the characteristics of your target audience. Then, **Write a script** for your video. Since you are promoting your business, you must be professional also in promoting your product. You may write even your agendas for your video as long as it will guide you in the whole process of your video making. Agendas such as grabbing attention and building interest must be included in your script. You may also use questions in your video to grab interest. Going back to our example about Fitness & Health, you may use questions such as: "Do you want to live a healthy lifestyle?" Then, persuade people through your script. You may include phrases why your product is effective or show pictures or clips that may support your business. After you write about how to persuade your audience, do not forget to include the most important part of your video. This is the call to action part of the script. You may include sentence like "What are you waiting for? Subscribe now!" or any tagline to implore the viewers.

You may now proceed with the **Recording of your video** after you have finished your script. Make sure that you are using the proper equipment and location for your video. Going back to our example earlier, you may use gym places for your location. Equipment such as a camera and a microphone may also affect the quality of your video. Make sure that you are using an HD camera while shooting your video. Choose places that have proper lighting. Doing so will avoid dullness for your video quality.

Editing the video also plays an important role in making an effective video Ad. Software such as: Sony Vegas, Camtasia or Screenflow are only few of the available video editing tools that you can use in creating a Video Ad. Remove any unnecessary scenes that you think will just be confusing in the perspective of the audience. Use relevant sounds for your Video Ad. If you are making an infomercial, use catchy sounds during the whole video to maintain the interest of the viewers until the end. Also integrate relevant texts for your Video Ad. Make sure that the data within the text are not too overwhelming to the point that the audience will struggle. Keeping the texts few and simple can successfully facilitate your Video Ad. However, if you are having a hard time in creating an original recorded video, you may use animated video format for your ads. These can be infographics and other pre-made video template tools that can be created via online sites such as Canva and Venngage.

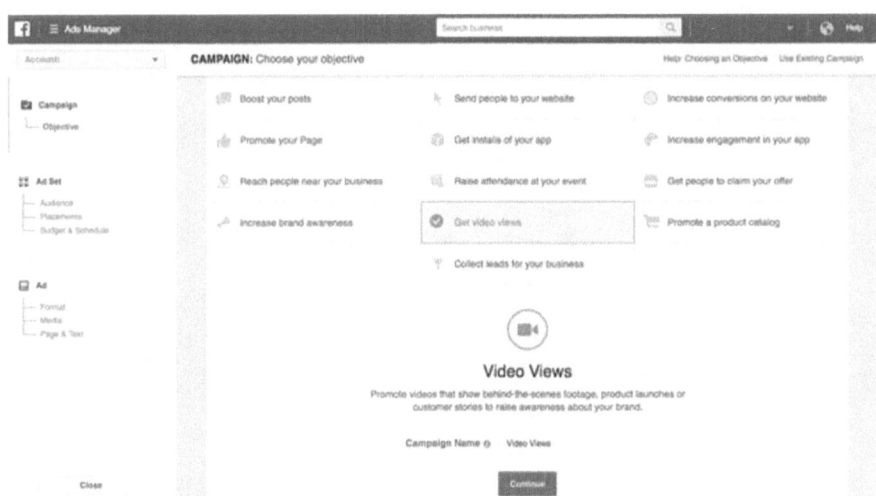

Figure 44: Get Video Views Campaign

After creating your video, **upload it** on the Ads Manager and choose the *Get video views* as your objective during the Campaign creation in order to track the results of your video ads later. Afterwards, your video ads may now be seen in desktop and mobile phones. The videos will play automatically in the News Feed of the viewers but muted. Keep in mind that the first 10 seconds of the video is key, so make it as catchy as possible. Attract the viewers, so they will unmute the video once they see your ad during the first 10 seconds. Take note that it is not a requirement to use the Get video views objective when using a video for your ads. You may still use different goals for your ads if you prefer to get results from other objectives rather than video views.

Part III – Ad Nurturing Essentials

Chapter I – Everything You Need to Know about the Facebook Advertisement Mechanism

1. What is the Ad Delivery System and How is it Being Optimized?

The *Facebook Ad Delivery System* is a system used by the platform to show your ads. This system determines the people who will see your ads, when they will see them, and where they will see them. The system based the audience during your ad creation. Since we've mentioned earlier about setting an audience in the Ads Manager, the system will automatically choose the audience who will most likely be related to the audience that you've chosen in the ad creation. If you have created multiple ads, Facebook will show each one at the beginning of the campaign equally. As time passes, Facebook will begin to show ads with the highest performance than the others. The system also knows that the longer it shows your ad, the longer they know its behavior such as the time that it performs the best. If you have chosen the "Optimization for Ad Delivery" objective in the Ad Set, you are telling Facebook to be efficient and get as many results as possible. Doing so will help you to analyze the results of your ad over time.

2. What is the Learning Phase?

If you're wondering what the learning phase of Facebook is, *the **Learning phase*** is actually the way the Facebook Algorithm works in displaying your advertisements. If you had setup your Audience or selected an objective, Facebook is learning how it will show your Ad to the audience for a certain period of time. The longer you have setup the Ad, the more optimized it can be. Thus, even if you change the budget, as long as Facebook already knows to whom the Ad will be shown, even if your reach became smaller, it still has a greater chance of winning a target audience since those audiences match the action you had initially input during the ad creation. You must remember that creating major changes in your Ad can reset the learning phase and cost per action can become more expensive.

The learning phase is most likely the way how Facebook thinks about to whom your Ads will be shown. It is important to remember to give time to Facebook to learn on how it will show your Ads. If the results are poor for the first few days even though you assigned the objectives properly, don't worry because Facebook is still adjusting. Don't try to restart or do major changes on your Ads in order not to confuse the algorithm during the Learning Phase.

3. What is Auction and How does it Work?

Ad Auction is a term used to refer to an auction that happens when a person is eligible to view the ad. Its sole purpose is to select the bests ads for the audience through its performance. The Facebook Ads that you have created will compete with each other during the process. Within the targeted audience. And not only your ads will participate in this competition, there will be ads of another advertisers within the targeted audience. Then, the Facebook System will determine who will win the auction.

If you want to see the competitiveness of your ad, we recommend that you raise your bid. Those bids that we are talking about are all cost control tools. Keep in mind that those with the highest bids doesn't win always. Facebook is also helping you in maximizing your ads so sometimes the bid with the lower cost wins. Facebook is in fact recommending you to enter your true maximum bid to ensure that you don't miss out any clicks or impressions on your ad.

The persons who are eligible to participate are those who are targeted for the ads to be shown. It works if the ad gets to perform well and with the highest total value. The total value doesn't mean of the costs of the Ad but a combination of 3 factors. These are: *Bid, Estimated Action Rates* and *Ad Quality and Relevance.*

Instances that can contribute to the total value can be ads that are not performing well. For example, if the ad received several negative feedbacks, it will decrease the total value. Besides, if the ads are shown to several people and they became interested to your business, then it will increase its total value. More about bidding will be discussed in later chapters.

Chapter 2 – How to Monitor an Ads' Performance Effectively

2.1 What are the 4 Basic Metrics You Need to Monitor?

Monitoring your performance is important in measuring the effectivity of your advertisements. However, monitoring is not enough since it is needed to be analyzed after. Monitoring and analyzing are two different things. In fact, monitoring only involves seeing the data and its performance but analyzing requires a study and comparison of the collected data given. You must also remember that not all data will be relevant to your campaign, which is why analyzing the data is vital. In fact, this reason justifies why some businesses hire an account analyst for the measurement of their ad results. However, as long as you know the math, you can do it by yourself.

There are 4 Ad Analysis Metrics that can help you in analyzing your Ad performance in the Facebook Platform during your Ad Set and Campaign creation.

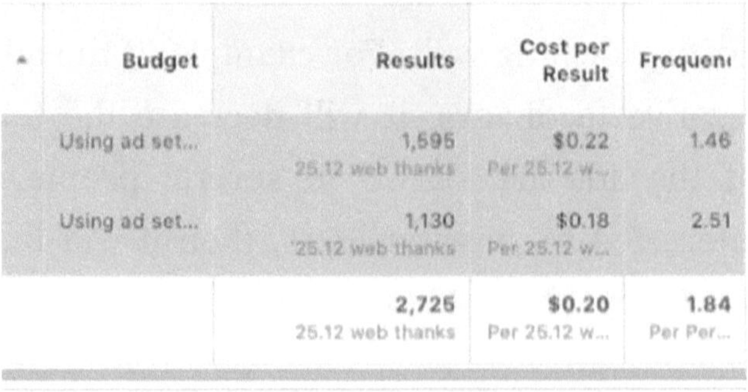

	Budget	Results	Cost per Result	Frequen
	Using ad set...	1,595 25.12 web thanks	$0.22 Per 25.12 w...	1.46
	Using ad set...	1,130 25.12 web thanks	$0.18 Per 25.12 w...	2.51
		2,725 25.12 web thanks	$0.20 Per 25.12 w...	1.84 Per Per...

Figure 45: Cost per Result

1. **Cost per Result** – This metric is the average cost per result from your ads. It means that it measures the cost-efficiency of your advertisements. It is assessed by the total amount spend divided by the number of the results you have obtained from your ads. The results depend on what you used for your advertisement such as clicks on your ad, impressions, video views and more. Using it will give you insights to compare it to the different ad campaigns you have made and see which areas still warrant improvement and the areas of opportunity. This metric can be influenced by several factors, depending on your input information such as the ad format used, target audience, and budget.
2. **Cost per 1,000 Impressions (CPM)** – This type of metric allows you to measure the cost-effectiveness of your ad campaign by the price per 1,000 ad impressions. It is calculated by the total amount spent on an ad campaign, divided by the impressions gathered then multiplied by 1,000.
3. **Frequency** – This estimated type of metric is used to determine the average number of times each person viewed or saw your Ad. It is calculated by the number of your impressions divided by the reach. The ideal frequency for an Ad is 1 to 2. However, there are times that frequencies give higher number especially if you had input bigger budget, audience size and schedule. Just remember that frequency is relevant to measure if the audience is seeing the Ads too often which may result to poor performance. Thus, if you see that your frequency

gets higher as time goes by, it is recommended to change your Ad strategies.

4. **Relevance Score** – Same as the frequency, this type of metric is an estimated type. Meaning to say, it measures the performance of your Ad by rating your target audience responding to your Ad from 1 to 10. It is automatically given by Facebook after your Ad receives more than 500 impressions. Unlike frequency, the higher your relevance score means that your Ad is performing well in reaching its audience, unlike other Ads. Facebook bases the relevance score on several factors such as: Ad performance, and Audience Feedback (Positive or Negative).

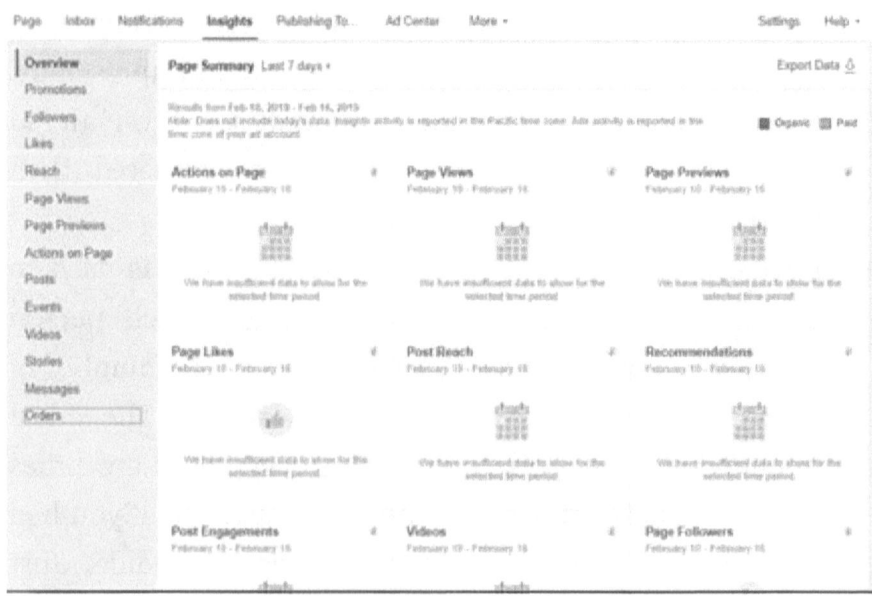

Figure 46: View Metrics

To view your metrics, it can be accessed through your Facebook Page. Above it, you can see an Insights tab. Make sure to click it to be able to view the metrics for your page. Several dashboards will be seen afterwards to give you an insight of your likes, reach and engagement. Metrics are automatically computed by Facebook and hovering through the charts will also deliver more information about your Ads.

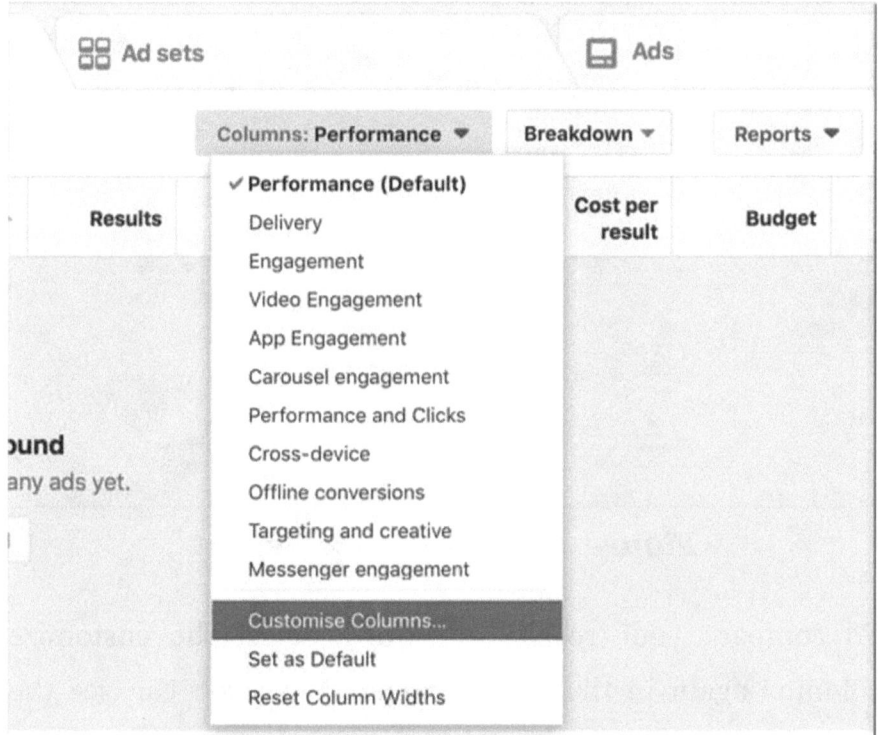

Figure 46A: Customize Report

You can also create a customized report through Facebook Ads Manager. By navigating the Ads Manager dashboard, select the customize columns in the columns drop down menu.

You may also remove any irrelevant columns that are checked in this category. Just select the metrics that you wanted to use for your ads such as Relevance Score, CPM and Frequency. Don't forget to click the apply button at the bottom to save any changes that you've done.

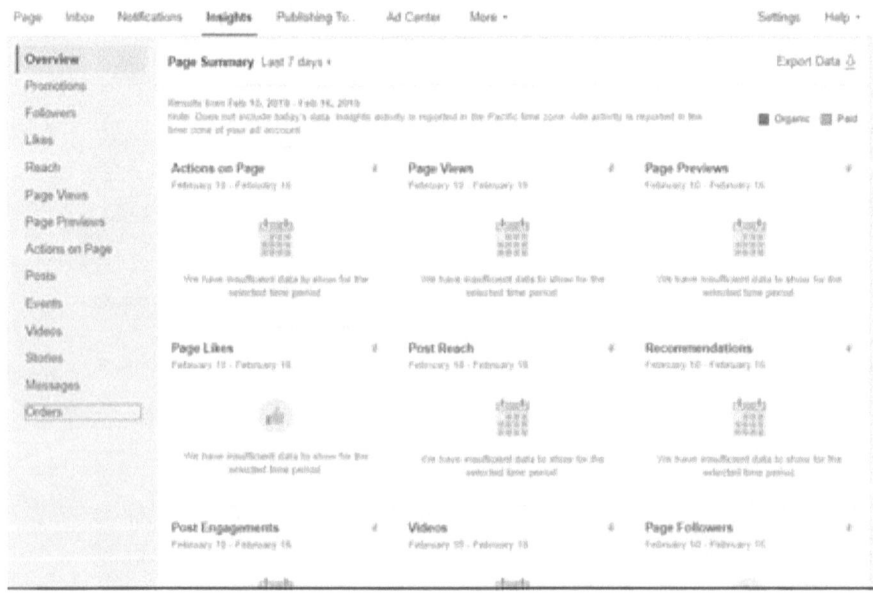

Figure 46B: Customize Report

To compare your results afterward, select the customize columns again in the Ads Manager. Now, you can see the reporting column for your Ad. Take note that you can rename the report: once that it's shown in the columns drop-down, it would be much easier to see. Compare the data by switching the dates in the reporting view. You may choose date periods like reports from last 7 days. Click the update and compare button then wait for the data. Your data will be shown afterwards and try to analyze the results if your ads are working effectively.

If you're wondering why some metrics are not available in your Insights tab because metrics are measured by how you budgeted and chose during your ad creation. If during your Ad set and Campaign creation, you formerly selected "Brand Awareness," then most likely, you will be charged per 1000 impressions which boils down to the CPM metrics mentioned earlier. On the other hand, boosting your page also gives you a metric for every post engagement you get from the audience. Make sure to choose your strategy appropriately during the creation of your Ad to see relevant data afterwards.

2.2 How to Use Breakdowns?

Breakdowns enable you to see the age of your audience, their location when viewing your ads and the devices that they are using. You may view this through the Ads Manager.

Alongside with the Columns dropdown that was mentioned earlier, the breakdown drop down can be seen. Click it. Then, you can observe several options for the breakdown. It is categorized by: *By delivery, By Action,* and *By time.*

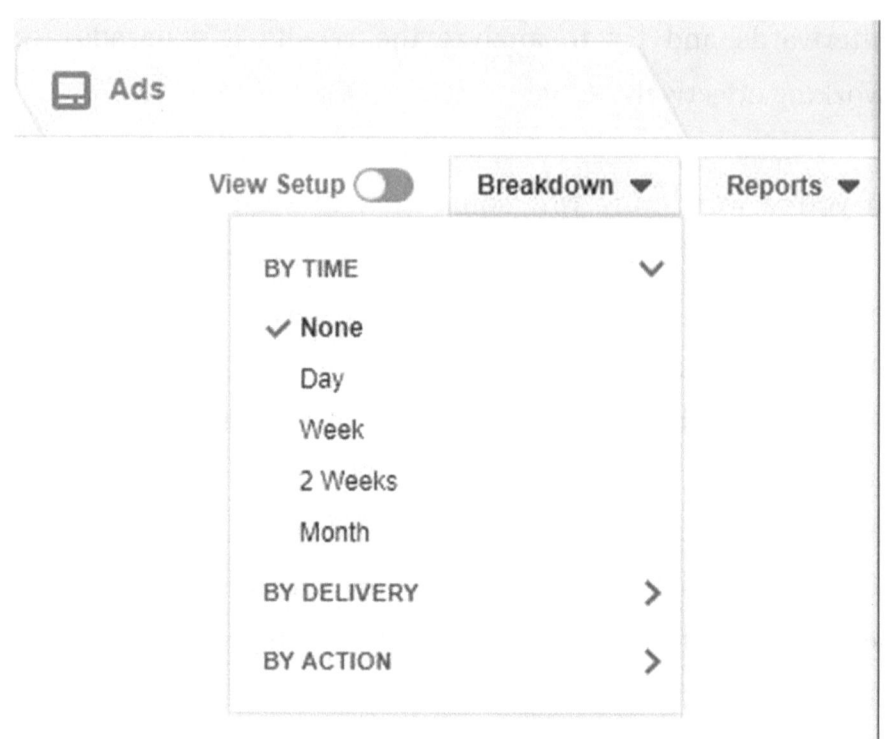

Figure 47: Breakdowns

Breakdown by Delivery – Selecting this category will enable you to assess more information about to whom your ads are shown. For example, if you wanted to see the age range of your viewers, select *Age*. Your results will display the age range of your viewers afterwards. You can also breakdown the results by location. Choose *Country, Region* or *DMA (Designated Market Area)* to analyze geographic information about your ads. The data will show where the viewers are located depending on how you have set up your location targeting.

Breakdown by Action – This category helps you to detect information about the actions of the viewers for your ads. Selecting it will show you how many clicks your ad received.

Breakdown by Time – If you select this category, it will deliver a more detailed report of your ads. It can be by day, week and months. Use this if you want to see when is the best season to use your ad.

Remember that you can combine several breakdowns to help you to analyze your ad results. For example, you can combine Age of your viewers and how many clicks they did under the Action. However, you cannot combine breakdowns under the same category.

Part IV – Troubleshooting Ad Performance

Chapter I – Types of Performance Issues

1. Ads are not Spending Enough

If you are facing this issue with your Ads, it means that Facebook stopped delivering your ads, or can't deliver it consistently because it's not competitive enough. Another reason is because it is not competitive in the auction. Earlier we mentioned about how bidding and auctions help you to analyze the performance of your Ads. Thus, Facebook might stop delivering your ads or might deliver them inconsistently because there are lower results for your target audience. If you noticed that all of your Ads are not performing well, you need to consider changing the entire look of your Ad or how you have setup the Ad Set or Campaigns.

To utilize your budget, make sure that your target audience is enough for your advertisement. Go back to the Audience settings by editing your ad through the Ads Manager, if you are having problem selecting an audience for your advertisements. Changing the type of Ad Campaign is also recommended if you determine that what you have chosen is not effective to your target audience.

2. Costs too High

This obstacle is the most common problem among advertisers. Lack of budget may hinder your advertising strategy. However, you must remember that if you want your advertisement to be effective, putting out enough capital plus your creative advertisements will lead you to success. Facebook depends on the budget that you have input. Optimizing your Ads through the budget in which you have input will still give you an advantage, instead of not budgeting for your advertisements at all. Keep in mind that not all expensive advertisements are effective. If you are in a start-up business, work with what budget you have. If your ad costs are too high, it is recommended to change the amount of budget.

By using the Ads Manager, go to the Ad Set or Campaign panel and click Edit. Make sure to confirm after you changed the budget to save any changes. Changing the budget will make Facebook re-learn on delivering your Ads, but it doesn't mean that it will restart the Ad optimization for your audience as long as you just make a small adjustment for your Ads such as changing the budget.

You may also use the "Optimization for Ad Delivery" choice for your Ad Set if you are having problems with high cost Ads. Doing so will tell Facebook to be efficient as much as possible in showing your Ads and will lessen the chance of getting high costs for your ads.

Chapter 2 – Changes You can Make to Improve Performance

2.1 Bid Strategy – Auction Issues

We have talked previously about Auctions and how they work. We also mentioned about bidding and how it is related to auction. To set your bid, you may edit this during the Budget and Schedule section of the Ads creation. Once you've clicked the Advanced Option, more settings about bidding will be shown.

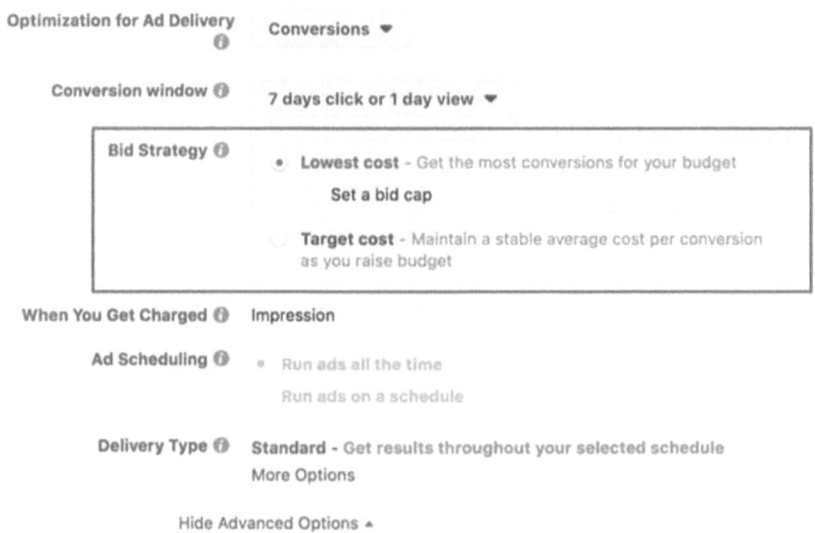

Figure 48: Bid Strategy

Thus, a term called **Lowest Cost Strategy** is used as a strategy to help you with some auction issues. This strategy tells Facebook to bid by having the lowest possible cost per optimization event, while also having to spend your budget wisely as the end of the day. If you want to maximize your budget, this strategy is recommended for you.

On the other hand, **Highest Value Strategy** is used to optimize Ad Sets for purchase value. This tactic informs Facebook to spend your entire budget for the end of your Ad Set schedule. Additionally, it works by also maximizing the amount of value you get from your purchases. For example, if a person made a purchase within 1 or 7 days, Facebook will try to maximize the amount of value generated from that person who clicked your Ad.

Another strategy that you can use is the **Bid Cap.** Bid Cap advises Facebook of the maximum budget for spending in an auction, which will also help you to decrease your costs. However, keep in mind that this is less flexible. Meaning to say, it can also impact the delivery of your Ad because bid caps limist what Facebook can do in every auction of your Ad. If you still want to set a bid cap, make sure to have more control over the cost per optimization event, rather than the budget. Because if the budget is too low, you may yield fewer ad results.

To set up the **Bidding and Optimization,** go to the Ads manager and click on the Columns Dropdown. Select the bidding and optimization option to get a report. A preset option is also available if you want to avoid certain issues in bidding such as report discrepancies. Remember that discrepancies are normal since Facebook's delivery system uses information differently.

2.2 Targeting – Audience Issues

Targeting an Audience is actually one of the most important steps to focus on when creating an advertisement. The reason why targeting is important is because not all the time your chosen target audience will be effective for your Ad. Targeting an audience requires caution as it may result to some issues that you may encounter later on. An issue that you might face is narrowing your audience too much in the Detailed Targeting section. We mentioned earlier how it can harm your Ad as it will not only reduce the results but also the way your Ad budget is being spent. To avoid this glitch, you must think of not too narrow but not too broad audience type that can help to increase the spending of your Ad. High quality audience might also reduce the cost per optimization event of your Ad.

Another issue that you may face is having an Overlapping Audience. However, it can lead to poor delivery of your Ad sets, because you may have set same target audience for your different advertisements. Facebook will only deliver the best performing ads and will prevent the others from being shown. You can check if the audiences are overlapping by going to the Audience section of Ads Manager and check the boxes of Ads that you want to compare. Click the Actions button then select the Show Audience Overlap option to see if your ads are overlapping audiences.

2.3 Creative – Ad Based Issues

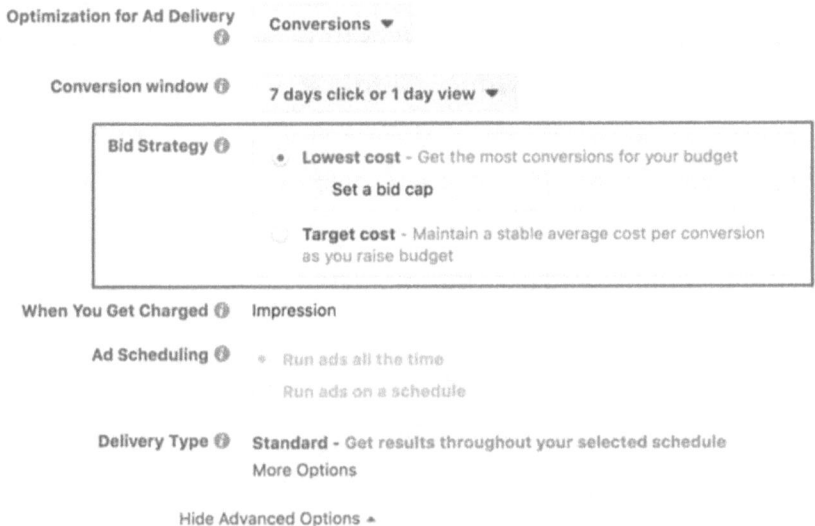

Figure 48: Creative Reporting

Creative Reporting is a helpful tool to address Ad Based Issues that you may encounter if your ad doesn't perform well with your audience. The report will enable you to analyze what ads can lead to troubles in budget spending. If you are facing Ad Based Issues, it also means that your ads are not effective enough to those audiences that are seeing it. In order to monitor this kind of issue, you may use the Creative Reporting in the Ads Manager through the Accounts Overview tab to see how your ads perform by creative unit. It will allow you to view various information types, such as impressions, results, and reach. It is more like a performance based report that may help you to analyze which ad is performing the best. For example, if you want to compare your video ad and photo ad, it is recommended to use this kind of reporting to ensure that your ads are effective enough for your audience.

Facebook also offers two products to help you with this issue. The first one is *Dynamic Creative*. This is a tool that generates a report from your Ads and how it relates with different audiences. The tool will also enable you to test what ad has the best result from each impression. The second one is the *Placement Asset Customization, which allows you* to customize the images or video you wanted to appear for each placement that you assign. It might be in different platforms such as: Facebook, Instagram, Messenger and Audience Network. You may also use this tool to change your assets, upload different video/image crops, and upload trimmed videos. The benefit of applying this tool will reduce the number of Ad sets needed for your Ad.

2.4 How to Chat with Support to Resolve any Issue

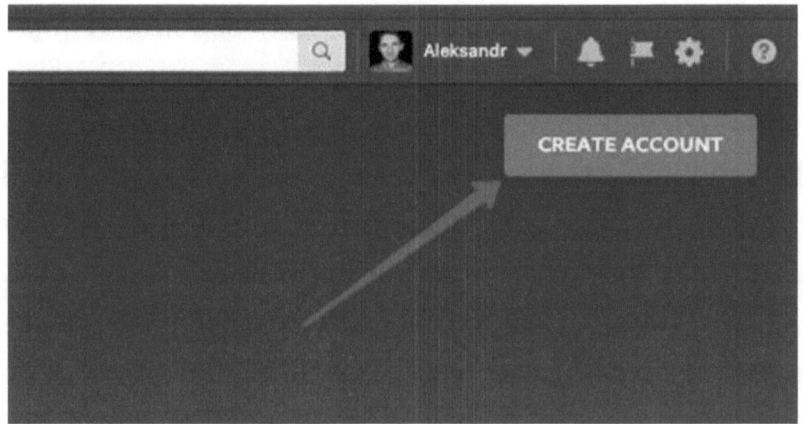

Figure 49: Help Button

Facebook tries to help its advertisers as much as possible. In fact, Facebook has released a Chat Support system in order to help them in their advertising issues. To resolve any issue and talk directly to Facebook, you may click the Help button at the right side of your Business Manager. It will reveal a task pane at the right side of the screen and then delivers three choices: *Contact your Marketing Expert, Ask Community* and *Support Inbox*. You must remember that these settings will only be available once you have an active billing account for your Business Manager. The first option is really advisable for beginners, especially if they are still confused of the process of Facebook advertisement. However, you still need to schedule a call before you can talk to the expert. Make sure to write all your questions or things that you want to know about before the scheduled call to lessen the hassle. The second option allows you to ask the community and receive answers from people who also experienced similar problems as yours. It is like a forum site, where you can ask and answer questions from different advertisers in Facebook. The third option enables you to get updates from the things that you've reported. Also, it facilitates you to see important messages from your Ad account, such as replies from the Help Team.

If you are having a problem with accessing the three options in your Ad Manager, click the "Still Need Help" button at the bottom of the pane so you will be redirected to the <u>Ads Help</u>

Center. It is recommended to use the Chat Support System if you need an answer right away. You can contact the chat support every Monday-Fridays 9am-5pm PST. If the chat support can't handle the issue right away, they will forward your issue to the appropriate Facebook Team concerning your problem.

Chat Support is broken down into several categories: *Billing & Payments, Creating Ads, Ad Performance & Delivery, Account Settings and Ads Management Tools, Reporting & Measurement, Pages & Instagram.* Select the category that is closest to your concern in order to be directed by Facebook to the correct support team. Remember that you must be logged in with your Ad Account with a current billing in order to use the Chat Support. If the Chat Support is not addressing your request, be mindful that they are only available during Mondays-Fridays and in business hours.

You may also use the articles provided in the Ads Help Center if you are having problems in contacting the Facebook Support Team through their chat support. The articles also cover topics such as Billing and Payments, Creating Ads, Ad Deliver and Performance, and many more.

Conclusion

Facebook Advertising is really an effective way of attracting potential customers. Thus, there are 5 important things that you must remember if you want to make profit by using Facebook Advertisement.

Facebook Ads Manager and Business Manager Set Up
The earlier chapters of this book mentioned about how you can set up your Ads Manager and Business Manager. It is vital to remember that these two are the fundamental parts of Facebook Advertising. Use what you have learned on the previous chapters to setup your Business Manager correctly. Remember to change your Timezone and Currency appropriately to avoid any billing conflicts. Also, if you want to be more organized in handling the accounts for your business, make sure to assign people who can help you in managing your Ad Account.

In terms of creating an Ad, the Ads Manager plays an essential part in acting as a central hub for your Ads. By selecting the Create button, you will be directed to the Campaign creation, Ad Set and Ads. Make sure to select the appropriate objectives based on the goals for your Ads. You may use reach, engagement, or other campaigns depending on the need of your ads. Also, choosing the right audience for your business is one of the most important aspect in creating an Ad. Remember to target the audience who will most likely be interested in buying your products. You may create a buyer persona for your business in order to guide you to the characteristics of your potential customers. Lastly, when creating the looks for your Ad, double-check to import relevant images or attractive images that can capture the eyes of your audience. Remember not to put too much words on an advertisement in order to balance the look of your Ads. Let the images/videos speak for your business. Also select the most effective Ad Placement and Ad format that you think will work for your particular business. Hence, to avoid having technical issues with regards to your image/video advertisement, you may visit the Facebook Ads Guide for the format requirements.

Working with a strategy using Facebook Funnel

We mentioned in the previous lessons the use of the Facebook Funnel Strategy. It is critical to know this strategy in order to convert your cold audience to warm audience. Make sure to target larger audience first and then slowly filter it down as time goes by to ensure that the audiences remaining have higher chances of buying your product. The Detailed Targeting setting and Lookalike Audiences may help you in targeting your audience using this strategy. However, make sure not too target too large or too narrow audiences to keep the balance of the viewers who will see your Ad. The five stages of the funneling also guide you in the process of creating your Ads. Also, remember to create an appropriate advertisement based on what Stage you are already in when using this strategy. This tip will help you to be more effective in promoting for your business.

Choosing a correct Goal, Audience and Creating an Eye-catching Ad.

When choosing the correct goal, you must think first about what are the things you would like to achieve for your business. If you want people to be aware of your product, use Brand Awareness. If you want to drive people to your website, use the Traffic Objective. It is important that you know what exactly the need of your business in order to still be aligned with your Ad objectives. Choosing an objective is one of the most critical part in creating an Ad. This may affect the results afterwards if not chosen properly. Be SMART (Specific, Measurable, Attainable, Realistic and Time-bound) with your goals. Questions such as: how long am I planning to run this advertisement or how many people do I want to reach are helpful when creating an ad. Just ensure that you are using the right campaign for your business in order not to waste money for the wrong objective.

Using the Ads Manager in targeting your audience is truly an effective way of advertising because the tool delivers flexibility in choosing your audience. We've mentioned formerly that you must not target too large or too narrow audiences, as it will affect the effectivity of your advertisement. Instead, you may think of the demographics of people that you want to reach such as their age, gender and location. Use the gauge that can be seen during the Ad Set creation in order to measure how many people you are going to reach if you place a certain budget on your ad.

Creating an eye-catching ad is the trickiest part of advertising because not all ads are pleasing to the eyes or engaging to viewers. We've also highlighted earlier about not putting a large number of texts on your advertisement. It is important to use images/videos that will give the viewers a glimpse of what your business is all about. Be realistic and original in your advertisement. Show only images that are related to your business and use call-to-action settings as much as possible.

Correct Analyzing and Monitoring Ad Performance

We've reiterated in the previous lessons about the importance of the 4 metrics. The 4 metrics are used in order to measure the effectiveness of the performance of your Ad. Above your Facebook Page, you can see an Insights tab. Make sure to click it to be able to view the metrics for your page. Several dashboards will be seen afterwards to offer you an insight of your likes, reach, and engagement. Metrics are automatically computed by Facebook and hovering through the charts will also give you more information about your Ads. Meanwhile, if you are using the Ads Manager to view the Ad Performance, you will see a chart setting at the right side of the Ads Manager.

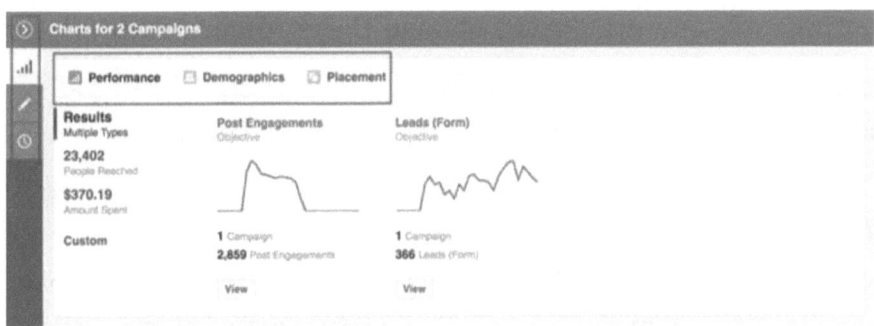

Figure 50: Chart Panel

In the side panel, you may click the Performance, Demographics and Placement if you want to see the charts for a specific campaign or Ad Set you have selected. The **Performance chart** will introduce you to the information of the audiences who selected your Ad and also, the total number of Reach for your Ad. Conversely, the **Demographics chart** shows how the Ad performs in the different factors such as age and genders. Lastly, **Placement chart** shows your ad's performance to the different platforms in Facebook, such as in Instagram and in Facebook itself. Individual results may also be seen for each of your advertisements in these panels.

If you are not into charts, you may also view the insights of your Ads in Facebook by going to the Ads Manager and clicking the Campaigns, Ad Sets and Ads Panel. Clicking these tabs will offer you insights on the number of people who saw your Ad, number of people who clicked your Ad, and the amount you spent in creating the Ad.

If you are monitoring regularly and noticed that your ads are not performing well, you need to consider changing the settings of your Ad. Try to change the Audience settings, or objectives of your Ads and monitor once again until you've seen an improvement of your ads' overall performance.

Effective Troubleshooting

Not all the time advertising is full of butterflies and rainbows. Sometimes, you'll face challenges in the field of advertising. Several issues you will face will test your endurance in the social media world. Thus, the last chapter of this book will give you practical tips on how to proactively deal with these challenges.

Know first what type of issue you are facing. It is easier to address issues if you know the root-cause of it. If you think that you can handle the issue, you may try to follow the things that we will be discussing. However, if you think that the matter is out of hand or you don't know how to resolve it, it is best to contact the Chat Support System or through the Facebook Ads Help Center to address your problem appropriately.

A challenge that you may stumble upon in your Ads is the issue of not delivering the Ad at all, or the ad is not performing well. Make sure to check several factors below that might help you in troubleshooting your Ads:

> **Ads Not Approved** – As listed in the past chapters, Facebook has Ad policies depending on the location, region, or country. Make sure to check and edit your Ads if the content wasn't approved by Facebook.

Paused Ad – Facebook doesn't show advertisements that are paused. To see if your Ads are paused, go to the Ads Manager and click the Campaign tab. Click the unpause button beside the campaign name of your Ad.

Spending Limit Reached – Facebook stops showing your Ad after you have reached your spending limit. You may reset and change your account by going to the Payment settings of the Facebook Business Manager, then click the Set Your Account Spending Limit button. Click the Reset button to input the Reset Amount Spent that you want to use.

Schedule – Facebook doesn't display Ads that are not on schedule. If you have chosen a schedule for your advertisement, make sure to check if it's already on schedule.

You may also get a help from a developer if you are having problems with embedding the Facebook Pixel to your website. The Facebook Pixel Helper tool may also be helpful in troubleshooting for your Pixel.

Advertising issues may be prevented if you choose the right strategy for your Ads. Budget, Creativity, and Audience are imperative in the overall effectiveness of your Ads' performance. Make sure to balance everything well to ensure that you gain the eyes of your target audience. Remember that your success depends on the response of those who will see your advertisements.

List of Terms

Account Spending Limit – allows you to automatically pause once you reach the limit you have set for your ads, unless you increase or remove the limit.

Ad Auction - is a term used to refer to an auction that happens when a person is eligible to view the ad.

Ad Banner - exemplifies a type of advertisement that delivers an Ad through websites.

Ad Campaign Goal – is used to tell Facebook your objectives for your advertisement.

Ad Set - denotes the place where you will assign the page (if you have multiple pages for your business), audience, placement, as well as the budgets & schedule for your campaign.

Ads Manager – is one of the essential tools in creating an advertisement in the Facebook Business Manager that can be seen under the Create & Manage page.

Ads Manager Guided Creation – reflects a recommended workflow for users who are new to Facebook Ads and wants to be guided step by step in creating their own advertisements.

Ads Manager Quick Creation – refers to a recommended workflow for people who are already familiar with Facebook Ads.

Bid Strategy – offers a tactic to improve the performance of your ads and how you would like Facebook to show your ads to the users.

Billing Threshold – works when you run your ads and accumulate an ad costs. It will start on an amount based on your chosen country and currency for your Ad account.

Boosted Posts – optimizes aspects in your Facebook Posts such as likes, comments and shares.

Breakdowns – allows you to see the age of your audience, your audience's location when viewing your ads, and the devices that they are using

Business Manager – delivers a free tool that helps you to manage your ad accounts, pages and also access for people you work with on Facebook.

Business Manager Partner – refers to those users from other businesses that you work with for your business, such as Ad agencies.

Call to Action Button – a feature that allows users to make an action such as clicking a button that tells the user to learn more or sign up through the ad.

Cold Audience – this type of audiences are those that are aware of your business but not ready to purchase your product.

Connections – term used to target your advertisement to people who are connected to the Page, App or Event in the Facebook Platform.

Conversion – a type of objective that aims to make people do a specific action such as signing up for an e-mail subscription or purchase your product.

Cost per 1,000 Impressions (CPM) – this type of metric allows you to measure the cost-effectiveness of your ad campaign by the price per 1,000 ad impressions.

Cost per Result – a term measured by the total amount spent divided by the number of the results you have obtained from your ads.

Daily Budget – specifies to Facebook the average amount you are willing to spend on a daily basis for your advertisement.

Detailed Targeting – provides a more detailed way of targeting people through demographics, mobile devices that people use & the speed of internet connection etc.

Facebook Funnel – reflects a strategy that will start first from having a broad target audience to smaller scale of people just like a funnel.

Facebook Pixel – an analytics tool available in the Facebook Business Manager that allows a user to see the effectiveness of the advertising by assessing the actions people visiting your website.

Frequency – an estimated type of metric which is used to see the average number of times each person viewed or saw your Ad.

Frequency Cap – denotes a way of keeping other people seeing your Ads too often.

Hot Audience – type of audience comprised of people who know your business and recognize what your products or services are for.

Lead Ads – ads used to collect information through newsletter sign-ups, business information, contact form and others.

Lead Generation – a type of objective that gathers contact information from people.

Learning Phase – is the method on how the Facebook Algorithm works in displaying your advertisements. The learning phase is most likely the way how Facebook thinks about to whom your Ads will be shown.

Lifetime Budget – set amount you are willing to spend in your entire ad campaign.

Lookalike Audience –are the type of audiences that Facebook reaches through your advertisement with the same interest as those people who are engaged in your business. Most likely, these are the people who are similar to your current customers.

Page Likes – is a term used to refer to how many likes your Facebook Page has gained from your advertisements.

Placement –is a term used to let Facebook show your Ads in the best places where they think your business will benefit much. It also refers to the places where you make your Ads run.

Post Engagement – tactic used to increase page posts attraction.

Reach - this type of objective helps you to boost the numbers of people that see your advertisements.

Relevance Score - measures the performance of your Ad by rating your target audience responding to your Ad from 1 to 10

Scheduling - allows you to control both the dates and times you want to show your Ads.

Timezone – a specific area or region that follows a certain time.

Traffic Objective – goal that is largely used when there is not enough audience for a conversion goal as it sends people to a destination on your website or page. It is more likely a substitute goal for the conversion objective.

Warm Audience - this audience type is comprised of people who somehow know your business and may interact with your business infrequently.

www.ingramcontent.com/pod-product-compliance
Lightning Source LLC
Chambersburg PA
CBHW030013190526
45157CB00016B/2695